WHY CHRISTIANS FIGHT OVER THE BIBLE

"*Dr. Newport has addressed himself to one of the major issues in Christendom today—how Christians look at the Bible. The issue is not the authority of the Scripture. It is how differing groups and perspectives interpret Scripture.*

"*Dr. Newport brings rich and cosmopolitan insights to illumine this perennial dilemma.*"

—WILLIAM L. HENDRICKS,
Professor of Theology,
Southwestern Baptist
Theological Seminary

WHY CHRISTIANS FIGHT OVER THE BIBLE

by John P. Newport
and William Cannon

THOMAS NELSON INC.
NASHVILLE / NEW YORK

Library of Congress Cataloging in Publication Data

Newport, John P.   1917-
  Why Christians fight over the Bible.

  1. Bible—Evidences, authority, etc. 2. Bible—Criticism, interpretation, etc. I. Cannon, William, 1918-
joint author. II. Title.
BS480.N43   220.6′6   74-4288

To all

who love the Bible

and regret

the controversy

over it

CONTENTS

PUBLISHER'S PREFACE

This book attempts to do the impossible—to give a brief but objective explanation of why Christian groups fight over the Bible. There is, as far as the Publisher knows, no other book currently in print that fills quite the specific niche for which this volume is intended. There are, of course, many books on the subject.

To be of the value desired for this volume, this book required a combination of deep scholarship, Christian dedication, and (a rather unusual ingredient) journalistic expertise.

Dr. John P. Newport, the author, is a man well-qualified to approach the formidable task of writing such a book as this. Dr. Newport's academic training and his professional background in biblical authority, biblical interpretation, and the philosophy of religion provide unique qualifications.

Dr. Newport's collaborator, William Cannon, has the necessary journalistic background and expertise to undergird the objective and neutral intent of the book.

The Publisher hopes that you will find the volume of value.

THOMAS NELSON, INC.

Why Christians Fight

Over the Bible

INTRODUCTION

In spite of the negative reaction of many Christian people to the word "fight," it is an accurate term to describe the actions and attitudes in regard to the Bible found among many Christians today. An outsider would not hesitate to designate that which is going on in Christian circles as a fight. Even more extreme language has been used. For example, Richard J. Coleman has used the term "theological warfare" to describe his understanding of the current situation.

Within the mainline Protestant denominations, seminary and university teachers, denominational officers, and even some pastors have their careers decided upon the basis of their real or alleged beliefs about the Bible. Nor is the controversy limited to the clergy. Lay persons oftentimes classify each other according to his or her view of the Bible, including its authority and interpretation.

Yet there is agreement. Most Christian groups in the Protestant tradition accept the Bible as the basic, if not the sole, norm of faith. Roman Catholics, also, since Vatican II, are putting increasing emphasis on the importance of the Bible. However, this agreement, even among Protestant groups, seems to stop with an abstract statement about the importance of the Bible. Different groups disagree on the nature of the Bible's authority and on how to utilize and interpret it.

Oftentimes, sometimes in an unconscious way, groups

are influenced by the founder of their particular group, or by some of the historic creeds. Even though the great Protestant Reformers affirmed that they were servants of the Bible, it is obvious that they worked from presuppositions and used many of the great creedal statements as aids in interpreting the Bible. For example, John Calvin, though he wrote the *Institutes* as a guide to understanding the Bible, was influenced by and followed the order of the Apostles' Creed. It is doubtful if Calvin was aware of any inconsistency here—if inconsistency there be. After all, although most conservative groups claim to be under the Bible (and sincerely cite such as a major point of superiority over the liberal position), do they not often-times judge what their teachers and leaders say on the basis of traditional and popular views or interpretations of the Scriptures? A neutral outsider—assuming that there can be such a thing as a neutral outsider—might be excused for concluding that, in fact, many denominational and confessional groups *appear* to feel that the view of the Bible and the interpretations expressed by their founders or early leaders are to be exalted (and in some cases almost deified). A group may fail to note that its creeds and historical confessions of faith are themselves historically conditioned. Of course, the founder or early leader *could* have been absolutely right, not only for his own time, but, theoretically even for the future. But should such a sweeping assumption be made?

Lest liberals gloat at such a state of affairs, it should be pointed out that they often enact the same drama from a different, but comparable, scenario.

There is an urgent need to keep the channels of communication clear and functioning in a healthy way between Christian groups. It is hoped that an objective study of the reasons Christians fight over the Bible will help in communication and dialogue. Oftentimes dialogue results in understanding, sharing, and mutual enrichment. The truth of God is always greater than any of our human statements of it.

When the author was in seminary, a popular idea was that the study of biblical languages and backgrounds would produce students whose interpretations were entirely free from presuppositions. In recent years, however, it has become obvious that no one studies the Bible without presuppositions. In fact, it is difficult to approach the Scriptures without a prior *theological* system in one's mind. Therefore, it is important, in interpreting Scriptures, for one to have an awareness of his own presuppositions as well as those of others.

Authority and Inspiration

As indicated above, most of the individuals and denominations in the history of Christianity have presupposed the authority of the Bible. And yet this presupposition has always been under scrutiny in Christian history. It was considered in a critical way first in relation to the problem of which books of the New Testament should be included in the Bible. (The Old Testament books had been discussed earlier in Jewish circles.) This problem became acute again in the Protestant Reformation, when the Protestant Reformers did not accept the Old Testament Apocrypha as valid for the canon or for doctrine.

Another dispute related to authority arose during the Reformation over Roman Catholic views concerning the relationship between oral tradition and biblical materials. The Roman Catholic view was crystallized at the sixteenth century Council of Trent. In the modern period, with the rise of the historical sciences and the impact of the natural sciences, the problem of the higher criticism of the Bible became a point of controversy.

A continuing area of disagreement among Christians is related to the "inspiration of the Bible." The Christian churches have always held that the Bible was inspired. However, the question of the *extent* and *nature* of the inspiration of the Bible was raised in the Reformation period and is still today a continuing point of disagreement. Even within conservative churches there is conflict. Some groups state that the Bible is infallible in all matters. Others say it is infallible only for faith and practice. Some argue that the Bible teaches a clear doctrine of verbal inspiration. Others affirm that a less dogmatic and more inductive approach to inspiration should be followed. In recent years a very controversial approach to the Bible has been the "Neo-Orthodox" view. Karl Barth and Emil Brunner, as well as other of its exponents, reacted against traditional orthodoxy. The orthodox view maintained that revelation was given as verbally inspired and communicated doctrine to the minds of the writers of the Bible. This the Neo-Orthodox rejected. For them, revelation is primarily an event—not a doctrine, nor a book. For the Neo-Orthodox, the Bible is a record of revelation, not the revelation itself.

At the present time there is much evidence that the "fight is on" over the matters suggested above—and over others. Denominational publications report battles within the denominational ranks over the inspiration and authority of the Bible. Denominational publications carry editorials—which oftentimes stimulate the battle.

Well-known pastors preach sermons concerning their views of the Bible, and, at the same time, criticize other views. The media tend to stir up the battle. They report the dramatic discussions and votes at conventions, assemblies, and synods. Even *Playboy* magazine recently carried an article by a prominent West Coast religious leader suggesting that the Bible is one of the most dangerous books in the world—at least (according to *Playboy*) in the way "Bible Belt conservatives" are using it. A glance at the Saturday church page in any representative metropolitan newspaper points up the conflict. As one sensitive theologian has said, "The Saturday religion section in the large newspaper is enough to chill the heart of any cultured person." Religious claims in these pages are oftentimes contradictory. In some cases they are so inane that they probably produce a tragic reaction in some readers' minds the sponsors certainly did not intend: they make agnosticism seem to be the only honorable refuge for an educated mind. No wonder Christians fight.

Books about the Bible are constantly being published with such words in their titles as "crisis" and "conflict." Some of these books are about the fight itself and provide an overview of the battle.

Slander by Label

Unfortunately, much of the warfare between Christian groups seeks to slander by label. Oftentimes the familiar terms "liberal," "Neo-Orthodox," "conservative" are not used in a way that would carry a clear and honest meaning. In some cases the descriptions are stereotypes and caricatures of the real beliefs of the persons holding them. Worst of all, careless speech oftentimes turns ideas into distortion. The result is a breakdown of communication and the development of tragic misunderstandings. Sadly, name-calling sometimes prevents open debate on serious issues.

Even conservative groups, thought to be firmly united

in preserving a conservative heritage, such as the Missouri Synod Lutherans, have been engaged in warfare over the inspiration of the Bible. In this particular controversy, the disagreement is somewhat different from the Fundamentalist-Modernist controversy of a number of years ago. No one engaged in the dispute disavows the authority of the Bible, but there is disagreement, for example, on the interpretation of the opening chapters of Genesis. The argument relates to whether or not factual inerrancy is an essential corollary of belief in the divine inspiration of the Bible.

For many persons on the outside, much of the battle seems to be a disagreement between ultraconservatives and moderate conservatives. For persons on the inside, however, such as the Missouri Synod leaders, the issues are far from minor: Lutheran theologians whom our theoretical neutral observer would see as relatively conservative have become liberals. The matter is no longer one of a minor nature.

In another prominent conservative denomination, a group recently charged that liberals have been infesting the denomination's colleges and seminaries. The term "liberal" in this usage is almost the same as "infidel." The word is as dangerous as the situation the group fears. In response, therefore, the more "progressive" elements in the churches of that denomination have preferred to refer to themselves as "Evangelicals" or "Moderates." The curious result is that even these formerly favorable words have become suspect.

Factors in the Battle

As will be seen, the direction of a man's religious thought often closely parallels his political thought. Theological liberals tend to align themselves with liberal social and economic approaches. Theological conservatives are oftentimes closely related to conservative social and economic patterns. Is this situation a factor in the animosity between the two groups?

There is the matter of church growth.

In recent years, conservative—and particularly Fundamentalist—churches have grown much more rapidly than have liberal churches. Liberals, in response to such growth, charge that the conservatives are superficial and primarily interested in quantity, not quality. The conservative answer is that the liberal churches are negative, vague, indecisive, and relative. Apparently sensing truth in such charges, liberals marshal their own array of invective. They say that many Fundamentalists and conservatives are humorless and ruthless, have little compassion, and allow the end to justify the means.

The battle is on!

But must it continue?

There is another group of Christians who suggest that there is a constructive alternative. This group, sometimes called "Neo-Evangelicals," suggests a solution to the conflict which, they claim, avoids the abuse of liberty arising from the extreme approaches.

In the meantime, Christians continue to fight over the Bible. The intent of this book is not to add to that conflict but, if possible, to diminish it. Hence the attempt in these pages to be as objective as possible. It is hoped that a study of the various contending groups will help each group to learn about the others. Each group has one or more valid insights. If such insights are presented fairly, this sharing and openness should cause a reexamination of presuppositions and a restudy of the Bible.

After all, the Bible, in all its power and grandeur, needs no defense. It needs to be studied, heard, and incarnated.

A word about the organization of this book.

The author intends to present a brief, neutral, simplified discussion, as non-technical as possible. The scholar will miss the footnotes to which he is accustomed; he is referred to the Bibliography, and his indulgence is asked in deference to the busy layman. Certain liberties have been taken in grouping points of view. Where it is felt that the practice would be helpful, terms are italicized. The use of journalistic subheads is for the same purpose.

CHAPTER ONE

Prejudice Begins
Many a Battle

Christians fight over the Bible for a variety of reasons. Usually they know why. But not always. Oftentimes, sometimes unconsciously, the roots of the conflict lie in deep-seated prejudices (or *appreciations;* prejudgment *can* result in right conclusions!) formed in their childhood or youth. In some cases such early life prejudices can be tragic; the person reacts *against* the influences to which he was subjected and closes his mind to the truths within them.

Let us consider a few specific examples.

One lady of the author's acquaintance has a psychological antipathy to—a deep-seated rejection—of the orthodox or conservative view of the Bible. She attributes this prejudice to the practices of her mother. The mother, who was a charming lady, had what would appear to be at first glance a very commendable attitude toward the Scriptures, what many would call a deep, childlike faith in the Bible. She saw no need to give study to biblical background. She felt it was perfectly proper to take verses out of context and use them to discipline the children. She frequently interlaced her telephone conversations with proof texts from the Bible used to absolutize her opinions—to make unquestioned proof of her point. Subsequently the daughter went away to college. There she was exposed to a more serious study of the Bible. The results were unfortunate. Later in life the daughter had great difficulty in accepting—or even being open to—a conservative approach to the Bible. Much of this attitude was undoubtedly a reaction to the views of her mother. Does her case parallel that of many? For example, can the eminent liberal preacher, Harry Emerson Fosdick, be understood in relationship to his reaction against the Fundamentalism of his childhood and of his early years in New York City? Tragic irony can create boomerangs; the views we seek to implant can come back to us in opposite form in our children.

On the other hand, there are those who have a wholesome appreciation for the Bible precisely because of the type of training they received in the home and because of the attitude which their parents had toward the Bible. Not all family discussion of the Bible during childhood, not all conversation about the Bible around the dinner table will produce a questioning attitude in a child's mind, a deep-seated scepticism in later life.

Influence of the Minister

It is obvious that some people fight over the Bible because of the influence of differing kinds of ministers in their background. That which a minister says oftentimes determines what a person believes.

The author knows one family whose members are very dogmatic in their understanding of "last things" because their childhood pastor, whom they admired very much, constantly spoke on the subject—in a dogmatic way. In fact, they say that the pastor indicated a person was not a true believer unless he accepted the specific viewpoint on last things preached by this pastor.

Unfortunately, some ministers have demagogic—or "ego trip"—tendencies. Their preaching emphasis is oftentimes influenced by selfish ambitions. They build up a following by criticizing other approaches to the Bible and other ministers who disagree with them. They sometimes develop in their churches a generation of people who believe that this particular minister's view is the only view, a generation that is quite bitter toward any other perspective.

Demagogic pastors can be either liberal or conservative. But the liberal pastor who usually comes to mind in terms of aggressive controversy is the one who criticizes conservative preachers as narrow and ignorant. Such "liberal types" have little to say about last things. They spend most of their time in relating the Bible to psychological and social issues. They usually have little understanding of conservative theological doctrine and have an antipathy toward anyone who holds this kind of viewpoint.

Cultural Surroundings

It is obvious that the cultural surroundings of a person will influence his view of the Bible. D. H. Lawrence, in his book *The Apocalypse,* expressed his reaction to the narrowness of his parents and of the church which they attended in a British town. Allen Watts, who has been a significant critic of conservative Christianity and an exponent of the Far Eastern religious perspective, was greatly influenced by his early background. While he was a young man in London, he acquired a considerable interest in non-Christian religions and no little aversion to conservative theology.

Many evangelical Christians grow up in a middle-class home and a middle-class church; they are never exposed to the more radical prophetic emphasis of the Bible. The author remembers a conservative pastor asking a state meeting of Christian leaders to forget the "social gospel" and preach the Bible. There was no recognition of the importance of the ethical and prophetic emphases in the Bible.

Rudolph Bultmann taught religion in a secular university setting in Germany. He was influenced by the fact that scientists and other critical scholars were teaching in the same university. He felt that he had to make the Bible acceptable to modern man, that the Bible was unacceptable unless scholars removed what Bultmann called "myths" from the biblical account. The influence of his surroundings on his teaching is very obvious.

On the other hand, men who have been educated in a denominational college and in a denominational seminary have not had to face many of the so-called secular criticisms of the Bible.

Theological Reasons for Conflict

Other persons fight over the Bible because of their tendency to follow and defend theological and practical traditions of their own fellowship or denomination. Practically speaking, most ministers and lay people support doctrines of their tradition, such as the security or insecurity of the believer, sacramental or non-sacramental significance of the Lord's Supper, sacramental or non-sacramental significance of baptism, and similar doctrines which were important historically in the establishment of the denomination. Consequently, there develops a particular approach to the Bible for each denomination or fellowship. But this particular approach may conflict with the particular approach of another fellowship. Therefore, in some areas there is considerable friction and controversy over the conflicting approaches and viewpoints.

The opposite may be true. A person may be reared in a denomination and have a reaction to the way in which doctrine was taught him by incompetent or dogmatic ministers or teachers. He sometimes develops an emotional antipathy toward the view of the Bible held by the denomination in which he was reared.

The degree and type of education which a minister or lay person has will oftentimes influence his attitude toward the Bible and his attitude toward other people's view of the Bible. Some facets of the current controversies over the Bible stem from the inevitable confrontation: those who hold a basically faith-oriented acceptance of the Bible at face value clash with their opposites, persons trained in the critical-historical method who base their beliefs on critical evaluations as well as faith. Whether one view is superior to the other is irrelevant to the obvious fact that the two will clash. And, lest it seem that education per se is always on the side of the critical, consider the following interesting fact: lay persons trained as secular scientists often react in a manner opposite to that of the clergy. Such lay persons are sometimes attracted to an organized, dogmatic, and literal approach to the Scriptures. The author found this response on the part of students at the Massachusetts Institute of Technology.

On the other hand, persons trained in the arts and literary understanding are often open to a more symbolic and less literal approach. The Harvard students are examples of this emphasis. It is significant that Martin Luther urged the young people in his time to study literature and poetry if they would have a proper understanding of the nature of the Bible. He emphasized that the Bible was written in the Middle East where people thought in dramatic categories.

Two Contemporary Dangers?

Neo-Evangelicals affirm that there are two contemporary dangers which hinder a proper understanding of the Bible. One is a mechanical literalizing, and the other is a demythologizing which seeks to minimize the dramatic or symbolic portions of the Bible. Roland M. Frye, an authority in literature, suggests that it was part of God's wisdom to raise up men who would record and preserve the Christian message in a semipopular, dramatic, and literary form. Frye further points out that, although the Bible is basically faithful to the events treated, it is also dramatic enough to reach a wide audience and to convey an indelible impression.

E. J. Carnell, the well-known conservative, laments what he considers the oftentimes rigid and intolerant mentality of Fundamentalism. He contends Fundamentalism wages a holy war against other persons' view of the Bible without admitting the elements of pride and personal interest that oftentimes prompt the call to battle. In some cases, such a mind set creates new evils while trying to correct old ones. For example, the Fundamentalist crusade against the Revised Standard Version of the Bible did not originate basically from a careful and scholarly study of that translation. The opposition seemed to have stemmed from the fact that there were Modernists on the translation committee. This meant, according to the logic of the Fundamentalists, that the translation must automatically be liberal and undesirable.

The liberal approach has its own problems. Oftentimes there is a built-in prejudice against conservatism which results in an unwillingness to be open to the evidence for the resurrection of Jesus Christ or for other significant conservative biblical doctrines.

On the other hand, some Fundamentalists are content with an educational system which substitutes piety for scholarship. They evidently feel that, if students are exposed to critical evidences concerning the trustworthiness of the Bible, their faith might be threatened. As a result, according to Carnell, some of the conservative students do not *earn* their right to believe and do not sense their deficiency. They sometimes gloss over negative evidence and deny that there are any difficulties in the Bible.

Summary

To summarize: *Differing influences in the religious pilgrimage* cause Christians to fight over the Bible.

But there are other reasons. What they are and how they interact will form the discussion of the following chapters.

CHAPTER TWO

MIND SET:
Cause for Conflict

Christians, like all persons, have differing psychological needs. Therein lies one explanation for some of the conflict over the Bible. Consider first the conservative.

Recent psychological studies indicate that the conservative mind tends to function best in a context of order and certainty. The conservative mind set has a low tolerance for ambiguity. Clear-cut lines of demarcation are appreciated. Self-confidence is a characteristic. Personal interest, which oftentimes colors decisions and viewpoints, is usually unnoticed. The conservative mind looks for a positive authority and has little appreciation for an ambiguous view of the Bible. The Bible becomes an anchor point—a place of safety and hope. This is particularly true in a rapidly-changing world. The conservative has strong feelings about security. To attack his conservative view of the Bible or his view of interpretation is to attack the very basis of life and security. He does not change easily. Even if he could be rationally shown that his view of the Bible is wrong or his method of interpretation is wrong, he would have difficulty in accepting such. His mind set would make it extremely painful for him to admit that he had been in error—perhaps for an extended period of time.

For example, John Calvin marshalled powerful criticisms of the Catholic use of the Old Testament Apocrypha (books written in the inter-biblical period) as sources of doctrine. Calvin pointed out that some of the significant early Catholic scholars, such as Jerome, admitted that the Apocrypha could be used for edification, but *not* for doctrine. Would the Catholic Church admit that it was wrong? No! It had used the Apocrypha too long. In the Middle Ages, before the practice was questioned, apocryphal material had been used for doctrine as well as education. The question came before the sixteenth century Council of Trent, called to deal with the Reformation challenge. It was very difficult for the Council to admit that, for probably four hundred years, there had been a wrong utilization of apocryphal material. The issue was never settled. Since the time of the Council of Trent the value of the Apocrypha for doctrine has continued to be a point of contention between Protestants and Catholics.

In like manner, present-day Protestant conservative views about the interpretation of prophecy, held for years, are not easily changed—no matter what the evidence.

"Face-saving" is important in the West as well as in the East. Some people feel that if they are wrong at one point they are wrong at all points. If the interpretation of one passage a person advocates is shown to be questionable, he may—if he follows the logic of this particular mind set—conclude that his biblical anchor has been destroyed. Is it any wonder that he will resist such an eventuality?

No one likes to be wrong—especially if he is told about it. This is obviously one factor in the conflicts that develop between lay people and college and seminary professors, as well as between theologians and pastors.

The Liberal Hang-ups

The liberal mind set, in contrast to the conservative, tends to operate with ambiguity. The environment is uncertain and complex. Contradictory data flows in from the media. For the liberal type, this situation does not constitute a major problem. He does not feel the compelling need to have everything absolutely certain in secular or religious matters. He can live with a certain amount of what he calls "reverent agnosticism." In fact, this type of person suspects anyone who *is* too certain, too dogmatic about his views. It is readily seen that such a person as the liberal would naturally argue with the person holding conservative views as to the authority and inspiration of the Bible. A literal approach to interpretation would also upset the liberal.

The Yale Studies in Preaching suggest that there is some correlation between a person's emotional and physical needs and his view of the authority of the Bible and its interpretation. This is not a static situation. Some persons remain at one level of understanding. Others work through successive need levels, changing beliefs or approaches at each level. For example, it is easy to understand how a nineteenth century slave would search out appropriate biblical verses portraying heaven as a static place of rest. On the other hand, sophisticated urbanites would find psychological satisfaction in passages indicating dynamic growth in heaven.

It has already been suggested that some persons from authoritarian homes long for freedom and adopt a more liberal view of the Bible and its interpretation to life. The opposite approach is oftentimes made if there is no security in the home. In this case, an authoritarian or dogmatic view of the Bible, along with a literal and highly organized interpretative system is adopted. The Jesus People in California, after their disillusionment with the drugs and the occult, had desperate security needs. They were essentially passive. Enroth's studies suggest that their conditioning in the drug world had made them "open" to things "done to and for" them. This applied to the acceptance of authority. A conservative and highly dogmatic approach to the Bible and its interpretation met their needs, and they embraced this approach eagerly. They have a heartfelt desire to follow the Bible to the last jot and tittle. Since they were disillusioned with society, they were especially open to a biblical interpretation that emphasizes that we are living in the last days. According to Enroth, Hal Lindsey's *The Late Great Planet Earth* has become a popular guide to their biblical interpretation.

Some persons, unfortunately, externalize and objectify the authority of the Bible in a static way. What was once God's confronting word, ever revitalizing and judging, becomes formalized and neutralized. Proof texts are found to support status quo opinions, positions, and prejudices. The Bible is no longer something to be *submitted to,* but something to be *used.* In some cases persons stand *upon* the Bible, rather than standing *under* the Bible.

In fact, some use the Bible in the manner of a demagogue. First, there is a statement about the terrible condition of things and the fact that there are heretics everywhere. Something must be done. Then, this demagogic type comes forward, stating that he is the last bastion of orthodoxy and that he is ready and willing to stand for the truth. By supporting his printed media— newsletter, newspaper, books, pamphlets, etc.—one can keep up with the real truth. The secular observer might conclude that such a demagogue's attack upon others might sometimes be with a deliberate distortion of what is said for the purpose of tearing that person down and building the critic up. In any event such an approach is an exploitation of the mind set of his listeners.

But there is more to the fight over the Bible than mind set. The next chapter explores another side of the coin.

Summary

To summarize: *Christians often fight over the Bible because of their differing psychological needs.* Oftentimes their approaches are thereby incompatible.

CHAPTER THREE

The Word Is "Practical"
But It Starts Fights

It is generally accepted that particular approaches to the Bible and particular portions of the Bible are utilized or interpreted in such a way as to undergird practical personal or group interests. (In other words, some persons may use the Bible for their own selfish ends, consciously or unconsciously. Others, not quite so blunt, may select approaches or interpretations that further a cause or a group interest.) Naturally these differing approaches and interpretations cause controversy.

The Protestant Reformer John Calvin left room in his writings for both conservative and the revolutionary approaches to the problem of the rights of civil rulers. There is strong evidence, however, that his interpretation of the Bible was weighted in the direction of magnifying the power and place of civil rulers and magistrates. There is also evidence that this emphasis was caused by a reaction to the revolutionary and nonconformist views of the radical Anabaptists of his time. They protested some aspects of Calvin's theocratic state in Geneva and fomented unrest in Europe. Calvin utilized and emphasized portions of the Bible such as Romans 12 which teach that the Christian is to be subordinate to the rulers or to those in authority.

One of Calvin's most devoted disciples was John Knox of Scotland. He came to Geneva to meet with Calvin after he was forced to flee Scotland because of unrest

and a non-Protestant ruler. Eventually John Knox returned to Scotland. Queen Mary was the Roman Catholic
ruler who opposed Protestant teaching. She was both
powerful and headstrong. There seemed to be no orderly
way to gain freedom for Protestant preaching and practices. John Knox decided to help organize a movement
to remove her from the throne. He was reminded that
John Calvin had taught that the Christian is to be obedient to those in power. Knox replied that Calvin's interpretation was formulated in reponse to the anarchial
Anabaptists. Therefore Knox, to meet his different practical situation, sought out those portions of the Bible that
called for opposition to a tyrannical government or ruler.
This is an excellent historical example of how equally
devout persons differ and argue over the Bible. The differing approaches of Calvin and Knox were influenced by
practical needs in each's particular situation.

If people are prosperous and comfortable, if they have
status in their present condition, they tend to use the
Bible to maintain the status quo. Paradoxically, some
persons who have a comfortable position in a society will
align themselves with leaders who teach an extreme other-
worldly view of the Bible, that these are the last days
of history and little can be done to change the social
order though many may be suffering injustice. In contrast,
minority groups and persons who feel they are being un-
justly treated by the social order use the same Bible to
justify radical approaches to social justice and to economic and social change.

Theodore Roszak is representative of the writers who
contend that the middle-class business community has
used Genesis 1–3 as a religious and philosophical base
for its right to subordinate—and even exploit—nature
for profit. According to Roszak, the Genesis teaching

that man is a sub-creator under God is used to justify exploitation of the natural resources of the planet.

In recent years, the counterculture leaders and those concerned with the ecological situation have used the Bible as a philosophical base to protest exploitation. They point out that the Bible teaches any sub-creating man does is to be *under* God, for God's glory and man's good. It is not to be for private financial gain. The counterculture individuals also point out that Jesus was more of an itinerant prophet than an industrialist. They note that He said the foxes have holes, and the birds have nests, but He had no place to put his head. They further note His interest in small children, the needs of the "down and out," and women. They add that He was not particularly concerned with material things. With such emphases it is not surprising that they have adopted Francis of Assisi as their model of one who rebelled against middle-class values and returned to the simplicities of nature.

Thus the Bible is used to undergird two different approaches to nature. Two groups take the same passages of Scripture and disagree in their interpretation. Each finds the Bible meeting its own particular practical need or interest.

At a recent national religious convention a resolution was introduced by a woman who quoted Ephesians 6:1–3 and Colossians 3:18–21 as proof texts for the idea that the man is to be the head of the woman and the children are to be subject to their parents. The quotations were accepted at face value. No one at the convention publicly attempted to see the passages in the context of the first century Middle Eastern view of women and children as subordinate within a patriarchial society. Another woman opposed the resolution, using as her proof text Galatians 3:28 to prove that men and women are one in Christ. She also quoted verses from Matthew 10:34–38 to prove that children should be ready to leave father or mother if necessary to follow Christ when there is a conflict. Two women. Two interpretations. One Bible.

Some women state that the Bible undergirds male chauvinism. Others are quick to point out that Jesus was one of the greatest liberators of women, that the Bible undergirds authentic freedom for women. Some see the ordination of women to be ministers as justified by Galatians 3:28. Others quote 1 Timothy 3:11–12 to prove the opposite.

It is widely known that some people in the American South have used biblical verses (such as the curse pronounced on Ham) as proof texts for supporting a supposed basic inferiority of Black people. On the other hand, their opposite members, civil rights leaders, have used the same Bible (but not the same verses!) to provide *their* proof texts in the fight for equality.

Karl Marx taught his socialist followers that biblical religion was an opiate to keep the oppressed masses in an humble and unjust situation by promising them better conditions in heaven. Harvey Cox, among others, has pointed out that in Africa, South America, and other underdeveloped areas the Bible is being used as the basis for a revolutionary demand for justice and better conditions for the masses.

George R. Beasley-Murray contends that one of the most powerful attractions of Communism is its teaching of hope. It promises the underprivileged masses that they will have better conditions here on earth in the utopian period beyond the revolution. This situation causes Beasley-Murray to call for a restudy of the millennial concept in the book of the Revelation. He thinks a neglect of this basic doctrine has left the Christian church powerless to confront the Marxists on the issue of a practical hope for mankind here on earth. According to Beasley-Murray, the Christian churches should take the book of Revelation seriously once more and recognize it as a Christian book containing authentic Christian doctrine. He points out that many eminent Bible scholars consider that this book teaches an earthly realization (at least for a period) of the triumphant kingdom which Christ will bring to pass at the Second Coming.

Beasley-Murray counters the objection from some that such a concept is Jewish by saying that would hardly be adequate grounds for rejecting the millennial teaching of Revelation. The book of Revelation is not "Jewish" in the sense of being sub-Christian. For Beasley-Murray, a renewed emphasis must be placed on Christ's Second Coming bringing into the world *then* with decisive expression the Kingdom that is present *now* in the hearts of men. Here is an example of a prominent scholar maintaining that a practical need for hope in our time demands a restudy and a reappropriation of a doctrine that some persons think is sub-Christian and should be avoided. He certainly has no selfish axe to grind, yet his approach to the Bible is practical.

Summary

Differing practical needs cause Christians to fight over the Bible.

CHAPTER FOUR

Christians Fight
When the World Changes

The world changes. That is, sociological changes occur periodically in any culture. Christians, like all people, react to changes in the society around them. But different groups have different reactions. For various interesting reasons such differing reactions lead to conflict over the Holy Scriptures.

Consider America.

In the history of the United States a pattern has developed. Each generation experiences a *cultural crisis*. (A similar situation exists in other countries.) These crises usually call for different approaches and utilizations of the Bible.

For example, in the 1960s in America, many Christians sought out biblical material which justified and undergirded social action. In the 1970s, however, the cultural crisis produced a renewal of interest in the more orthodox and private approach to the Bible. Now, conflict has arisen between those who accept the social emphasis popular in the sixties and those who are "turned on" by the new orthodox emphasis.

The top religious news story in America today, according to religious news editors, is the dramatic trend toward conservatism. Even some liberal background Christians are joining the growing parade! Is it not ironic that at the very same time social action liberals flock to the conservative standard, a group of some of the country's outstanding conservative leaders should meet to consider a call for more social action on the part of *their* churches? This national meeting (in Chicago) adopted a document which states that, from their conservative perspective, faith and social concern are inseparable. Rauschenbush is turning over in his grave!

In the sixties, conflicting Christian groups utilized the Bible to support opposing positions in regard to racial unrest. Some Christian groups believed that the principles taught in the Bible justified demonstration. Other groups contended that the Bible called for submission to those in authority. Generally speaking, in the North and the East the Bible was used to back up and undergird the freedom marches. In the South the same Bible was often utilized to play down or oppose the same freedom marches. (Generalizations are risky at best, but the broad outlines hold.)

Woman's Liberation

Consider the role of the Bible in one of the dramatic social developments of recent years, the call for woman's liberation. Recent meetings of the American Academy of Religion have featured sections on woman's liberation. Long papers have been read setting forth biblical justification for the woman's liberation movement. Such major theologians as Karl Barth have been vigorously criticized as being "male chauvinists." The world does change!

On the other hand, *conservative* forces have rallied behind the Basic Youth Conflicts Seminars. These seminars have seen as many as a quarter of a million people a year gather in auditoriums to hear Bill Gothard state that the Bible establishes a "chain of command." This "chain of command" means: (1) the man is to be subordinate to God; (2) the woman subordinate to the man; (3) and the children subordinate to the parents.

Such large religious groups in America as the Episcopal Church have encountered opposition to the attempt to approve the ordination of women. The argument is used that the biblical materials (as well as precedent) are negative. Some conservative denominations (example: the Southern Baptist Convention) are beginning to ordain women to the ministry. This is being done in spite of what some think is Scriptural opposition in 1 Corinthians 7 and 1 Timothy 3. Taken at face value, apart from the context, these passages suggest that a woman is to be quiet in church or is not to be a teacher. (Note how the controversy here hinges on the *interpretation* of a passage.)

Tighten the Reins!

In a changing and increasing pluralistic society, many people use the Bible to tighten the reins. John Warwick Montgomery contends that the Missouri Synod Lutheran leaders have been turning their backs on biblical orthodoxy in an attempt to break out of their immigrant church background and be more related to the broader theological world. Montgomery himself has become an apologist for a conservative biblical perspective that would tighten the reins of those who would break out of the traditional orthodoxy of the Missouri Synod Lutheran Church.

The Millennial Issue—and Prophecy

Although there are many other factors involved, sociological changes have influenced the approach taken toward the millennial problem and prophetic Scriptures. Fifty years ago, *postmillennialism,* which said there would be a "golden age" established upon the earth by the

supernatural power of the gospel, a golden age preceding
the return of Christ, was very popular. Eminent orthodox
leaders such as Warfield and George W. Truett taught
that Christ would not return to earth until *after* the
golden age—or millennium—had been established upon
earth. This golden age would be established as the result
of the work of Christ through His church.

This postmillennial interpretation of the Kingdom was
shaken by two world wars, a worldwide depression, and
the veritable incarnation of satanic evil which the present
generation is witnessing. To take its place as a popular
view, there arose among conservative scholars an interpretation which is called *"dispensational premillennialism,"*
or *"pre-tribulationalism."* This new view arose out of a
prophetic awakening in the early nineteenth century in
England under the leadership of John Darby. Darby
was very disillusioned by the deadness and formalism of
the organized church and the ordained ministry. He
developed a method of interpreting prophecy which was
pessimistic about the power of the Kingdom until the
return of the Jews and the Kingdom Age. As for Christendom and the church in general, Darby taught that God
had already forsaken them. Believers are to forsake the
order of man which has corrupted the church. They should
assemble in simple unity.

Many factors were involved in the development of
Darby's viewpoint. However, the sociological factors in
Darby's England—and later in the United States—
undoubtedly influenced the rise of this dispensational
method of interpreting the Bible.

E. J. Carnell, of Fuller Seminary, himself a historic
premillennialist, suggests that dispensationalism in practice often honors the distinctives of Judaism rather than
those of Christianity. He states that the dispensational-

ists have withdrawn from general theological dialogue and thus have few active checks upon their method of interpreting the Bible. Carnell contends that their method of interpreting the Bible violates some of the most elementary canons of biblical hermeneutics. Example: One such rule is that the Old Testament must be interpreted in the light of the New Testament and not vice versa. For the sake of comparison, an interesting study would involve an analysis of the factors which led many former dispensationalists such as Carnell, George Ladd, and Daniel Fuller to forsake the dispensational approach and develop the mediating approach called *"Historic Premillennialism."* One clue is found in the importance they give to the "Olive Tree Analogy" in Romans 9–11, which teaches the unity of God's people and purpose.

Summary

But to return to our thesis and summarize: *Changes in the society create new needs in biblical interpretation. The differing reactions of Christians to such sociological changes inevitably produce conflict.* So we have another reason for Christians to fight over the Bible.

CHAPTER FIVE

"What Is Truth?"
Causes Bible Fights

Here we get into deep water—the ultimate nature of truth and reality. But we are examining the reasons Christians fight over the Bible, and this is one of them. It may not be apparent, even to the participants in the struggle, but differing views of conceptualizing the ultimate nature of truth and reality have caused many a bitter battle. While it may seem strange that such an abstract, philosophical question as is raised by the sentence, "What is truth?" could matter, the resulting conflict is far from abstract. So, let us examine a few instances.

Conservative Rationalists

Conservatives tend to cast thoughts into "either-or" and antithetical categories. This is sometimes called the "*Conservative Rationalistic View.*" John W. Montgomery, Clark Pinnock, and Francis Schaeffer are usually classified in this category. They utilize an "intended apologetic," basing the case for Christianity on a criterion held in common with unbelievers. Gordon Clark, a spokesman for this view, contends that the laws of logic are universally valid. A statement is either true or it is not true. If I have a proposition or idea on one side that is true, which is contradicted by an idea on the other side, logically the second idea must be false. Applied to theology, this view states that there is a sharp distinction between the infallible Word of God and the fallible words of man.

It can be seen that the Conservative Rationalist has a mind set for clearly contrasting ideas. It is almost impossible for a person of this temperament to speak of relative truths. In fact, it is the task of theology, according to this perspective, to bring man's relative thinking into conformity with the absoluteness of God's revelation. An air-tight rational system is to be desired.

Francis Schaeffer, a well-known advocate of this view, contends that the Conservative Rationalist is rational, but that he is not rationalistic. He thinks and acts on the basis that "A is not non-A." There are only two views of life, and they are logically irreconcilable. One view states that everything in the universe, including man, can be explained in terms of the impersonal plus time, plus chance. The opposing view states that the answer to the problem of existence is found in the teaching that the infinite-personal triune God is there and that He has spoken in Christ and the Bible.

Dialectical Liberals

The liberal mind set tends to cast thought into "yes and no" or dialectical categories. This view usually separates the Christian faith and rational categories. Truth is never a simple matter of "either-or" but results from contrasting one statement with another in order to seek a higher synthesis of opposites. Applied to the theological realm, the Bible is seen as both the Word of God and the word of man. In both cases, the two statements are true in themselves. When combined, however, they produce a higher truth. This type of mind set appreciates paradoxes and dislikes straight-forward statements or an over-simplified approach.

Viewed from the liberal prospective, the "yes and no" approach is the appropriate form of conceptualization in regard to the Bible. This type of thinking affirms both the divine infallibility and the human fallibility of the Bible. The Bible gives "infallible information" concerning God and his purposes, and yet it is susceptible to error in its historical, scientific, and even theological statements. Neo-Orthodox theologians such as Emil Brunner and Karl Barth are representatives of this view.

The Lutheran scholar James Kallas suggests that the Hebrew mind thought paradoxically because it thought in terms of verbs instead of nouns. In such paradoxical thought, opposites can stand together in tension. From the perspective of Kallas, if a person would rightly understand the Bible, he must learn to think like the Hebrews and hold opposites together in tension. Was Jesus human or divine? Is man determined or free? Is the Bible both divine and human? The dialectical view affirms that both are true.

An even more extreme version of the liberal mind set sees Biblical truth as incomplete and relative because it is filtered through human finiteness. In fact, human finiteness and relativity are absolutized to the point that Divine revelation is limited in its importance or clarity. Theologians under the influence of Existentialism go so far as to say that truth is almost completely determined or colored by human perception and response. The Bible is little more than a book which helps to bring men to authentic understanding and a knowledge of personal, existential truth.

It is not surprising that the Conservative Rationalist and the liberal mind sets are in constant disagreement and controversy. How much of the substance of these viewpoints is based on biblical revelation rather than on psychological and social conditioning is a matter of controversy in itself.

A third alternative is sometimes called the "New

Evangelical mind set." This group has been described as having a "both-and" mind set in regard to the Bible. The "theological" or "faith and practice" truth of the Bible is said by this group to be infallible. In historical and scientific matters, however, the Bible bears the marks of cultural conditioning.

Another characteristic of the Evangelical perspective is that the Bible is seen as both conceptual and experiential. It is both propositional and personal. The Bible gives cognitive and adequate knowledge, but it does not provide perfect knowledge in non-theological details.

The Evangelical approach views reason as being involved in the Fall. Therefore, there must be an inward spiritual change before rational apologetics can have much value. After the spiritual change, a Christian world view can be worked out which has profound rational implications and can stand as a model for judging other world views.

Summary

To summarize: For two persons to understand each other, they have to speak a mutually intelligible language. Given the fact that one group of Christians starts from one basic premise concerning the nature of what is true and what is not true, and another group starts from a view that is totally different, it is inevitable that neither group will be able to understand the other.

Unfortunate, perhaps, but true.

Let us move on to easier matters.

CHAPTER SIX

Differing Views of
The Meaning of Authority

All Christians accept the triune God in self-revelation as the final authority. The channels for the mediation of that authority, however, constitute a basis for controversy. For example, the traditional Roman Catholic approach teaches that the authority of God is mediated to men not only by the written Bible but by oral tradition. The unwritten channel of authority came from Christ and the apostles in an oral manner. It has been preserved through the Roman Catholic hierarchy culminating in the Papacy. In fact, Protestants understand the traditional Roman Catholic theory of authority as the church, and ultimately the Pope. Although the Bible is a part of the pattern of authority, the final spiritual meaning of the Bible is to be interpreted in accordance with the teaching of the church. Protestants, on the other hand, accept only the written word as authoritative. Progressive Roman Catholics have given a greater emphasis to the authority of the Bible in relation to oral tradition since Vatican Council II.

A further point of controversy involves the fact that the Roman Catholic Church uses the Old Testament Apocrypha (largely written between the time of the Old and New Testaments) as a basis not only for edification and inspiration but for doctrine. The Protestant churches use only the sixty-six books of the traditional Bible. Jesus apparently refrained from quoting and using the Apocrypha, as did the apostles.

Within Protestant ranks, at least three views of the meaning of authority constitute the basis for continuing and considerable controversy.

The Conservative Position

The *traditional conservative position* affirms that God reveals Himself in concepts and propositions that are direct and objective. Because this revealed truth, enshrined in the Bible, is supernaturally revealed, it escapes the time-bound character of most knowledge. The biblical writers were guided to write down the right thoughts and right words.

Revelation, which constitutes authority, consists of a combination of divine events such as the Exodus and the resurrection of Jesus and a corresponding interpretative word given to prophets and apostles. God revealed objective truths about Himself.

Most conservative scholars allow critical and historical approaches to the Bible within proper limits. It must be remembered, however, that the Holy Spirit inspired the biblical writers in a way which enabled them to transcend their cultural environment when speaking God's Word. God conferred a distinctive absolute to their words which keeps men from making them relative. Many conservatives suggest that Neo-Orthodoxy and liberalism have opened the door to religious skepticism and subjectivity in their neglect of the objective and direct nature of the Bible. Men need a timeless standard in Scripture to test false revelations.

The miraculous character of revelation is important because it serves to point to the power of God. God's power sometimes cooperates with normal human activity in the concursive inspiration of the Bible writers. At other times it assumes more dramatic form in the unusual events of the day of Pentecost. This power of God authenticates His message. It also speaks to man's abnormal condition of blindness and ignorance occasioned by sin. These signs of revelation in the cosmos also prevent a wrong use of human subjectivity.

The Bible produces a metaphysical system of thought which offers a coherent and consistent picture of the world. All men do not accept this system because neither their hearts nor wills have been changed or regenerated. The Bible has authoritative content. God has chosen not to reveal himself apart from historical truths and conceptual ideas. There is a firm line between that which comes from God and that which comes from human reason. Friedrich Schleiermacher, for example, is wrong, from a conservative perspective, because he championed an experience-centered faith lacking in objectivity and the conceptual.

The Liberal Position

The *liberal position* finds itself in essential conflict with the conservative teaching about the Bible. For the liberal, authority is relative and subjective. The Bible, along with all conceptual thinking, is conditioned in a cultural, historical, and sociological way. Authority and revelation have their beginning in the biblical period. However, they are progressive, open-ended, and partial in nature. Wolfhart Pannenberg of Germany makes this emphasis in his writing.

Revelation is not the divine communication of universally valid propositions. This would lock revelation into the thought patterns of a particular age and be too narrow. Rather, authority and revelation come as men respond to God's disclosure of Himself as reported in the Apostolic church and the Bible. H. Richard Niebuhr gives a classic exposition of this view in his writings.

Revelation is a guideline event of God's self-disclosure which results in a new orientation in thought and life. The Exodus and the resurrection of Jesus were such guideline events.

Instead of being direct and objective, the liberal claims that God reveals Himself indirectly and nonobjectively. For example, the crossing by the Hebrews of the Red Sea (or Sea of Reeds) appears in Exodus 13 and 14 to have involved God's direct intervention in holding back the flow of the Red Sea. Utilizing *Form Critical* methods, the liberal scholar thinks that what actually happened is different. The Hebrews, on foot, went through the muddy marshlands of the Sea of Reeds at night. They waited until Pharaoh's heavily armed chariots became trapped in the mud. Panic set in, and the Egyptians were routed. Later, the Hebrews enlarged the story, and God was pictured as holding back a great sea. Eventually the actual mud event was overshadowed by an emphasis on God's miraculous intervention.

For the liberal, the Hebrews saw, with the eyes of faith, within the natural processes of life and history something of what they expected God to do in the light of His promises to Abraham. The victory over the Egyptians and the escape became revelatory for the Hebrews. They saw their history in a new light as a result of this experience.

Revelation, for the liberal, can be from God without being confirmed by awe-inspiring acts. The important thing is the truth of the content revealed. God can reveal Himself without objective breaks in historical, natural, or psychological processes. God's revelation is thus indirect and closed to objective, scientific proof.

Authority and religious truth are located, for the liberal, in the relative and the historical. This truth is not complete, but it is sufficient for salvation and as a general guideline for action. Revealed truth, though from God, cannot escape historical relativity. When it is put into the words of the biblical times, it is put into a limited cultural form conditioned by that particular age. An example would be the biblical teachings about women and slaves. The substance of the faith is changed as the church sees more fully the implications of the original revelation.

According to the liberals, the biblical authors did not substantially misrepresent God by the ancient literary and cultural forms they used. These forms, however, are not absolute. They need development. The supposedly unchanging truth, "God is love," now takes on new meaning in the light of new knowledge of history, psychology, and philosophy. Later development adds new insight, precision, and understanding.

For the liberal, the Bible has no objective authority until the Holy Spirit makes the human words become the Word of God. This point is emphasized in the rewriting of the Westminster Confession of Faith in 1967. The Bible is neither unique nor authoritative in its own right. The Bible *becomes* the Word of God as it is received and obeyed under the guidance of the Holy Spirit in a subjective, present, ever-new word of revelation.

This view, says the liberal, avoids making the Bible a static book. It keeps God's Word a confronting Word which continues to revitalize and judge. The conservative view, according to the liberal, institutionalizes and neutralizes the Bible and allows it to be used as an authority for radically different opinions and positions.

According to the liberal, the conservative as a static view tends to see the Bible as something to be used—not the dynamic basis for change and submission to God which was its original intention. The objective and literal approach encourages arbitrary proof-texting for evidence while other evidence is passed over, artifically harmonized, or played down. An example of such a use of the Bible was the defense of slavery on biblical grounds. For the liberal, the Bible is not an objective rule book or dictionary.

The Evangelical Position

A third view is sometimes called *New Evangelicalism.* It is seen by some as a mediating view. It affirms that authority is both objective *and* subjective.

God's revelation is dependent on a personal relationship to Christ in order to prevent it from becoming mere assent to a set of cold and impersonal facts. It is also conceptual so it can be verified and distinguished from false teachings.

The critical-historical method is accepted by the New Evangelicals with proper limitations. It can throw light upon the cultural and historical background of the Bible, but it cannot lay hold of the divine significance of the text. A certain amount of relativism helps in understanding the Bible in the light of its particular age. Unrestricted acceptance of relativity is avoided since it would destroy all norms and impair the Bible's authority.

For the New Evangelicals, such as Ronald Nash, the Bible is the word of man as well as the Word of God. The divine Word is made through a human word that bears the mark of cultural conditioning. It was God Himself, according to John Calvin, who condescended Himself by using human modes of thought and speech in order to be understood by mortal man. Although these historical forms prevent us from knowing God totally, they do not falsify or misrepresent God in any way.

It is also true that some error will attend all Biblical

exegesis because all interpreters are sinners and prompted by personal interest. This fact is why Carnell states that New Evangelical interpreters must submit their partial insights to discussion within the communion of saints. Free and open conversation is needed.

New Evangelicals affirm that there is a basic difference between the historical form of revelation and its inner, objective substance. The historical form reflects the particulars of the age in which it was written. The New Testament talks about the details of female attire and the problem of giving a virgin in marriage. The biblical writers, however, inspired by the Holy Spirit, transcended their cultural environment to give essential and definitive religious truth. This truth centered in Jesus Christ. In a systematic teaching form, such as the book of Romans, central theological teachings are given in the Bible which serve as a criterion for evaluating that which is peripheral. The divinely inspired teaching or doctrine apart from historical matters is seen to be infallible and without error rather than *everything* reported in the Bible. This doctrinal message is available to man only by the Holy Spirit.

The living Word must not be set against the written Word. The Bible is the Word of God and also contains the Word of God. The Bible discloses the divine person (personal) and the divine will (propositional). This is an important balance to be maintained. The apostles were appointed to render a normative doctrine as well as call for a personal experience with Christ.

Ronald Nash and Bernard Ramm, among others, claim that this evangelical view of authority is different from and superior to the views of both traditional conservatives and liberals. It combines an *objective* divine revelation *with* the eternal *subjective* divine witness. This view avoids the error of subjectivism, relativism, and scepti-

cism, and also avoids the wrong kind of "wooden" objec-
tivism. There is a divinely inspired intelligible and verbal
Bible to be appropriated in a personal and intellectual
way. Liberalism depreciates this evangelical view in its
zeal for humanistic creativity.

Evaluation and Summary

All three views of authority discussed above are perhaps
overstated for emphasis. Out of the controversy between
these Christian groups, however, valuable lessons can be
learned.

Conservatives can learn that God is a God of truth, and
the Christian should not be afraid of facts—even when
they are related to the Bible. An unhealthy dualism between revealed truth and human truths should not be
allowed to develop. Some see a credibility gap between
the conservative claims and the evidence it presents. Pre-
conceived limits for biblical studies should not be set. It
would be good to live with the rough spots and natural
tensions encountered in approaching the Bible as a historical document rather than trying to smooth them out.
There should be courage and readiness to think something
through to the end, come what may, in regard to the
Bible.

Another truth neglected by conservatives is' related to
the fact that eternal truths must be experienced truths.
This does not mean a loss of content. Creativity as well
as defensiveness, however, is needed by conservatives.

Liberals also stand to learn from the arguments and controversies with the conservatives. In their attempt to
humanize the gospel and keep it from being static, they
have over-subjectivized the Christian religion. The normative biblical truths about Christ's person have been neglected in the almost formless "I-Thou" encounters.

Liberals can also learn the limits and dangers of a completely independent critical-historical method. There is a theological limit to the authority placed on the conclusions of the critical method.

An emphasis on the uniqueness and unity of the Bible is needed by liberals to balance their emphasis on the diversity of the Bible and its similarity to its surrounding cultures. John Bright, the eminent Presbyterian scholar, has already learned this lesson.

CHAPTER SEVEN

Is the Bible Inspired
And Without Error?

Unless it could be the problem of last things, no other subject is as controversial as the inspiration and inerrancy of the Bible. At this point, there continues to be a conflict among Christians.

The Classic Liberal Position

The *classic liberal position* states that the Bible is a *human* witness to divine revelation. The roots of this position are found in the liberal teachers of the German universities, especially in the early part of the twentieth century. As a product of the Conservative "Bible Belt," the author was first exposed to an "authentic" liberal position in a British classroom in the person of an Old Testament professor trained at Berlin University. Later in New York City, the author was exposed to a "radical" New Testament form critic also trained in Germany.

It must be said, in all fairness, that recent years have found a more restrained approach, even among the so-called "liberal" biblical scholars. This is in reaction to the more radical approaches of earlier years. Today there are *post*-Bultmann scholars, Salvation schools, Pannenberg followers, and the Uppsala school of Sweden.

Nevertheless, the liberals say that they cannot go back to an old conservativism. In fact, liberalism was born as a reaction to a doctrine of Scripture that externalized the divinity of the Bible. Source criticism, historical and literary criticism, and textual and comparative studies convinced most of these scholars of the dual or triple authorship of Isaiah, the composite nature of the Pentateuch, and the pseudonymity of some New Testament books. Liberals found evidence of redactors shaping and coloring the material for theological reasons. The liberal spotlight brought out every blemish in the conservatives' divine book.

An early forerunner of the modern liberal critics was the Old Testament scholar, Henry Preserved Smith. He engaged in open controversy with the conservative leader, B. B. Warfield. He challenged Warfield's central thesis that the biblical expression, "It is written," means that "God says it." Using 1 Corinthians 3:19, Smith pointed out the reference to the speech of Eliphaz in Job. And even the most conservative scholars admitted that the speeches of Eliphaz were not inspired. Smith went on to search the Old Testament for troublesome and seemingly contradictory passages. Where 2 Samuel 8:4 lists 700 horsemen, 1 Chronicles 18:4 numbers 7,000. Whereas 2 Samuel 10:18 says that David destroyed 700 Syrian chariots, 1 Chronicles 19:18 sets the figure at 7,000.

In more recent years, Warfield's favorite biblical verses proving inerrancy are said to be themselves conditioned in that they were late developments in the early church as it sought to protect its faith from error. Markus Barth, for example, in *Conversation with the Bible,* uses nine pages to show that the Fundamentalists misuse and distort 2 Timothy 3:16, "All Scripture is inspired of God." Markus Barth claims that this verse does not say that words or books rather than persons are inspired by God's Spirit.

For these liberal scholars, each strand and tradition of the Bible came from a different historical and geographical setting and expressed a particular point of view. The

creation account in Genesis 1 and Genesis 2:4a is set
against a background of watery chaos. The second account in Genesis 2:4bf is set against a background of dry
desert. The style of the unknown Yahwistic writer is full
of joyful confidence and concerns itself with God's selection and promises to Abraham; it stands in relief against
the style of the writer of Deuteronomy. The Isaiah of
Chapters 40–46 already knew a destroyed Jerusalem. This
is quite different from the eighth century background of
Isaiah, Chapters 1–39. As for the New Testament, there
is no static unity. It represents a variety of theological
positions, according to Käseman, the well-known German
liberal scholar.

Turning to the conservative position, the liberal has a
critical word. He contends that the biblical authors could
not have had the Holy Spirit choose just the right words
for them and yet still choose their own words. If the biblical authors were controlled, why is there such a diversity
of style, language, and thought?

The liberal questions how the biblical writers could be
"culturally conditioned" and still be inerrant and verbally
inspired. How can the Bible take on historical forms and
still be perfect? For the liberal, biblical concepts and
myths are bound together and, so, are conditioned by
time. The Bible is primarily a book to awaken self-understanding—not convey infallible information.

The liberal also wants to differentiate between those
parts of the Bible which directly witness to Christ and
those which witness to Christ only indirectly, some very
indirectly. There is a canon within the canon.

For the liberals, the prophets, Jesus, and Paul were
themselves opposed to a static doctrine of inspiration.
Each felt free to preach the gospel in his own way.

The heart of inspiration, according to James Smart, is

not in the text of the Bible, but in the dynamic relation between the interpreter and the Holy Spirit. Scripture remains a human book, the words of fallible men, until the Holy Spirit enables us to find and see the word of God which is contained therein. The text is important, but the crux is the work of the Holy Spirit through the human words.

Karl Barth and other Neo-Orthodox writers qualified the liberal thrust. They spoke much of revelation and very little of inspiration. Barth is an exception and even includes the words of the biblical authors in the event of inspiration. Yet he has been reluctant to affirm that inspiration guarantees a fully reliable and true account of the works of God in biblical history.

Barth affirms both the divine infallibility and human fallibility of the Bible, but it is not clear exactly what he means by these terms. On the one hand, Barth declares that the Bible gives "infallible information" concerning God and His will and His purpose for the world. On the other hand, Barth states that the Bible is susceptible to error, not only in its historical and scientific statements, but also in its theological statements. He seems to mean that when the Bible is taken as a whole, it gives a reliable and trustworthy picture of God and His gospel. When a text is treated only in its limited context, however, its interpretation is inadequate or deficient and needs to be supplemented. Barth also appears to have in mind that the biblical writers, being wholly human, were conditioned by their cultural and historical backgrounds. This means that they were incapable of seeing the whole truth from their particular vantage points. It could be said that, for Barth, the Bible is functionally adequate in that it is capable of bringing to men the truth of the gospel but that it is not necessarily dependable in everything that it reports. It is basically truthful and authoritative despite its external flaws. Barth opposes the theory of verbal inspiration as traditionally stated because in his view it freezes the Word of God in human propositions. It is obvious that Barth prefers to reinterpret inspiration in dynamic terms, making a place for the Spirit's guidance of the writers but also including the reception of the Word of God by the readers.

The Conservative View

The *traditional conservative* view of inspiration has followed the early leadership of B. B. Warfield and Charles Hodge. New Evangelicals find Warfield "straddling the fence" between the "perfect expression" and "fully sufficient" views. The traditionalists follow, however, the teaching of Warfield that emphasizes the Bible as the perfect and errorless recording of God's exact message.

Warfield and Hodge contend that inspiration communicates truth as divine authority. The biblical expression, "It is written," means, "God says it." And whatever God says is true because He says it. Warfield states the inspiration by the Holy Spirit saw to it that the biblical authors gave us the Words of God which are perfectly infallible.

"Plenary and Verbal" are two key words in the traditional conservative view. Verbal inspiration asserts that the writer's words, as well as thoughts, were "breathed out by God." For Charles Hodge, all the books of the Bible are equally inspired, and inspiration extends to all the contents of the several books. Verbal inspiration is seen as a necessary corollary to conceptual inspiration. The right thoughts cannot be expressed without the right words. The Holy Spirit, says Pache, influenced the biblical writers to set down in exact and authentic words the message of God.

The logic of the traditional conservatives is that the Bible is correct concerning all matters or none at all. Plenary and verbal inspiration necessitates inerrancy. As indicated above, Warfield's view is that the Bible plainly testifies to its own inspiration and inerrancy. Furthermore, the Bible itself has external marks which prove its inspiration.

W. A. Criswell develops these two approaches in his book *Why I Preach That the Bible Is Literally True.* He points out the internal witness to inerrancy in the teachings of Christ and other New Testament books. External marks, such as the literal fulfilment of prophecy, the confirmation of archaeology, and the organic unity of the Bible, are cited.

In *Biblical Revelation,* Clark Pinnock gives an exhaustive statement of the biblical verses that require infallibility and inerrancy. These include 2 Tim. 3:16, 2 Peter 1:20, 21, Matthew 5:17, 18, Mark 7:13, Psalms 18:17, Isaiah 45:19, Proverbs 30:5, 6, and Romans 15:4.

It is clear that traditional conservatives build their chief case on biblical passages which connect inspiration with truth on divine authority. For Warfield, the contemporary Christian should accept the same view toward the Scripture as Christ. For Christ, "It is written" referred to matters of doctrinal truth, practical duty, historical fact, and verbal form.

If Christ and the apostles are our authorities, maintains Warfield, their view of the Bible as infallible must be accepted. Either the apostles are bearers of doctrine or they are not. If they are, then the church must accept their teaching on inspiration. If they are not to be trusted, then Christianity has no objective authority. The liberals, maintain Warfield, would lead Christianity to a whole new view of inspiration and theology. For Warfield, it meant that the liberals raised the perennially old question, whether Christianity is based on what the Bible teaches or what men teach.

The liberals modified the traditional doctrine of inspiration by raising up difficulties. In doing this, said Warfield, they forfeited the principle by which *any* Christian doctrine is established. The result is a loss of an objective norm. Instead of debating particular difficulties, Warfield rested his case on biblical statements about inspiration. For Warfield, it was: *Infallible Scripture or Infallible Science.*

In all fairness, it should be said that traditional conservatives since Warfield have made a fair and honest effort to harmonize the Bible's doctrine of inspiration with inductive difficulties raised by liberals.

W. Arndt and Pache have written in this area. W. Arndt's *Bible Difficulties* is subtitled "An Examination of Passages of the Bible Alleged to Be Irreconcilable with Its Inspiration." In no case, however, do traditional conservatives accommodate their doctrine of inspiration to the difficulties.

The New Evangelicals

New Evangelicals follow the leadership of the English theologian, James Orr. For Orr, the communication of *life*, not knowledge, is the goal of inspiration. The Bible has the qualities claimed for it as an inspired book. It leads to God and to Christ. Furthermore, it gives light on the deepest problems of life, death, and eternity. It shows to men the way of deliverance from sin. It makes men new creatures. It "furnishes" the man of God completely for every good work. Biblical verses are cited by Orr that link inspiration with power to communicate life in Christ. Inspiration, says Paul, confers on Scripture the properties of being profitable for teaching, reproof, correction, and instruction which is in righteousness. The Scriptures have the power to make men wise unto salvation through faith which is in Christ Jesus. Of similar nature are the qualities ascribed in the psalms to the law of God such as "restoring the soul" and "making wise the simple."

For Orr, it was not fair or wise to try to avoid inductive difficulties. The problems should be acknowledged. In *historical* matters, the Bible writers depended on the ordinary channels of information such as older documents, oral traditions, public registers, and genealogical lists. The claim made is that the sources of information are good, trustworthy, and not that inspiration lifts the writer above the need of dependence on them. Where sources of information fail, or where, as may sometimes happen, there are blots or misreadings of names or errors of transcription, it is not to be supposed that supernatural information is granted to supply the lack. Orr contends that where this is frankly acknowledged, inspiration is cleared from a great many of the difficulties which have been attached to it.

Since the purpose of inspiration is to communicate life in Christ, Orr contends that this purpose is reached whether or not the Holy Spirit corrected the documents from which the Chronicler in the Old Testament drew his information. God does all things perfectly, but the standard of this perfection is the will of God, not the will of man. The Chronicler, for example, is inspired to make us wise unto salvation, and not to supply us with an infallible review of Semitic history.

E. Y. Mullins and other conservative authors in the 1920s and '30s were greatly influenced by Orr's view.

Another more contemporary exponent of New Evangelical views, in the tradition of James Orr, is Daniel P.

Fuller of the Fuller Theological Seminary. Fuller suggests a corrective to Warfield which would not change the basic outline of Warfield's argument. It would limit, however, inerrancy to those statements that are able to make men wise unto salvation. Fuller notes that the doctrinal verses which Warfield used always teach or imply infallibility in connection with revealed knowledge. They are not used primarily in connection with knowledge which makes a man wise to botany, or cosmology, or paleontology. Infallibility does not apply to this knowledge which is non-revelational simply because it is readily accessible to men. It is obvious that Fuller is arguing that inspiration and inerrancy are two different matters. Proof texts for inspiration are not necessarily proof texts for inerrancy. According to Fuller, the Bible does not, strictly speaking, teach plenary inerrancy.

In order to communicate His truth in revelational matters most adequately, God accommodated Himself in non-revelational matters to the way the original readers viewed the world about them. Fuller follows Calvin in this emphasis.

Everett Harrison, also of Fuller Theological Seminary, provides certain guidelines for discussing biblical truthfulness from a New Evangelical perspective. The Bible must be interpreted and judged in terms of its own usage and intentions. It must be seen according to the standards of meaning and accuracy employed in its day, rather than by twentieth century standards. When the Bible speaks of natural matters, it is using phenomenal language rather than scientifically precise language. It simply describes an event the way it would appear to the human eye. Thus the sun is described as rising and setting because that is how it appears to the eye. No error is involved here. The Bible's use of numbers and time is not very specific in many cases. To demand closer specification of time would be to interpret the Bible in a fashion foreign to its cultural setting, and thus to treat it unfairly.

It is also important to seek to get at the exact meaning of terms, states Harrison. If the Bible speaks of someone as a son, it may not mean a male first-generation descendant, but simply one possessing certain qualities. It should also be noted that the Bible is a progressive revelation. The degree of completeness and exactness was proportional to the degree of spiritual maturity of the recipients of the revelation. Early passages, consequently, do not give the same amount of detail as later portions. Many of the apparent errors in Scripture appear erroneous because of a misunderstanding of what Scripture involves.

The majority of New Evangelicals would prefer the terms "adequate" or "fully sufficient" to the term "infallibly perfect." Ramm insists that the idea of inspiration did not bestow on the writers a twentieth century mind. Nor did inspiration serve to smuggle into the text a timeless world view. Rather that special revelation came to a particular man, living in some particular culture, and speaking some particular language, and written in some particular literary form. God accommodated His revelation so that it could enter our world and be understood. On many occasions, John Calvin spoke of the great condescension in which God lowered Himself that He might be heard and understood. Both Calvin and Ramm are saying that only partial, but adequate, knowledge of God is given to man because it must always be mediated through human words and historical forms. In other words, verbal inspiration means that the Bible is trustworthy for our salvation but not necessarily infallible on all historical and scientific matters.

For Donald Bloesch, who has written concerning the New Evangelicalism, Scripture is the infallible norm for faith and practice. It is the inspired record of God's revelation and His divinely appointed medium. Inspiration means that the Scriptures have God as their primary author even though they are also the product of men who lived in a particular time and place. The writers are real authors, and the words and imagery that they employ therefore bear the stamp of cultural relativity. But it is in and through these culturally conditioned words that God speaks His eternal, unconditioned Word. The Scriptures present to us the Word of God in the concrete speech of a particular people.

Inspiration always conveys the truth that the writers were guided in their selection of words and meanings so that their overall witness is reliable and trustworthy. By virtue of its divine inspiration, the Bible can be regarded as an adequate and normative expression of God's will and purpose. Yet, according to Bloesch, its manner of expression often shows the taint of human weakness and infirmity. The truth of revelation did not drop from heaven but was discovered in significant encounters and occurrences in the crises and trials that confronted the people of Israel. The eyes of the prophets and apostles were opened by the Spirit of God to the divine significance of the crucial events of their times.

When New Evangelicals say that the Scripture is the infallible rule for faith and practice, this must be taken to mean the Bible as a whole and interpreted by the Spirit. Any text when not seen in its spiritual and theological context becomes an occasion for misunderstanding and sometimes deception. When New Evangelicals affirm that the Scriptures do not err, they mean that whatever Christ teaches in the Bible is completely true. Scripture is without error in its matter. This means: in its basic teaching and witness.

Even among New Evangelicals, there is an inner tension between upholding a high view of Scripture and doing justice to the historical-human dimension of the Bible. This cleavage is partly a reflection of the biblical text itself. The passages on inspiration are apparently too rich and variegated to be comprehended under the limitations of any single theory.

New Evangelicals are agreed that inspiration is not an end in itself. Its value is instrumental. It is intended to bring the reader into a certain relationship with the God who stands behind it. The Bible is never to be reverenced or worshiped, as an end to itself, and it is not to be conceived of as having some magical or automatic effect.

There is an additional element involved in the Bible's functioning as an authority which is oftentimes called *illumination*. The ultimate authority, according to Ramm, is the Holy Spirit speaking in the Word. As the Bible is read, the Holy Spirit works in such a way as to bring to the reader an understanding of the Word, and thus a conviction of its truth. There is a pattern of authority: the written Word (external) and the witness of the Spirit (internal) which together constitute the voice of God.

According to the New Evangelicals, the Bible is objectively the Word of God, whether anyone is reading or hearing it, and whether one is actually encountering God in the Bible or not. This is stressed in a number of ways. Ramm contends that the Bible is divine revelation in written form. Its words are, when properly understood, what God would actually have man to know, understand, and do.

The New Evangelical insists that the words of the Bible are objectively true, and that, correctly understood, they have one definite meaning. Illumination conveys understanding of the meaning and persuasion as to its truth. Presumably this meaning would be the same for anyone receiving the illumination.

Despite the differences between the traditional conservatives and the New Evangelicals, it should be said that the New Evangelicals have no problem about quoting the Bible with a sense that this is what God actually intends man to know. The problem of determining the meaning may be still present, but, for the New Evangelicals, there is an objective truth.

Summary

Liberals, conservatives, and New Evangelicals have different understandings of both the inspiration and the inerrancy of the Bible. Since both inspiration and inerrancy are basic and crucial to any system of biblical belief, obviously there will be strong conflict.

CHAPTER EIGHT

The Thorny Question
Of "Language"

Christians fight because they have differing views of religious language, biblical language in particular. (In this context, "language" is used in the sense of expressing thought and conveying information. If you are a layman, check your dictionary.)

The Bible has been under far more serious attack during the last few decades than many people realize. An important forerunner of the recent attacks was David Hume. In one of his critical essays, *An Enquiry Concerning Human Understanding*, written some two hundred years ago, he contended that any statement, to be meaningful, must be either rational (logically self-evident) or subject to the control of the five physical senses. His judgment was that, if a religious book could not meet such tests, it should be "committed to the flames."

In more recent years, beginning soon after 1920, a group of scientific men on the continent of Europe called the "Vienna Group" rigorously criticized all religious and theological statements. Ernst Mach, an important man in the movement, advocated a unification of science and mankind through the elimination of consideration of metaphysical and religious statements. The Vienna Circle insisted that theological statements were meaningless since they could not be brought under the control of the physically observable. About 1930, the term "Logical Positivism" (or "Logical Empiricism") was coined in reference to the Vienna Circle and this viewpoint. Later the term was extended to other Continental scholars and to some British philosophers such as A. J. Ayer.

A movement called "Linguistic Analysis" had its historical origin in G. E. Moore's essay, "The Refutation of Idealism," which appeared in 1903. Moore attacked the Idealists and the religious people because they tend to sacrifice clarity and preciseness. He defended the view that the primary business of a philosopher was language analysis. The most important man in British analysis is Ludwig Wittgenstein (1889–1951). His early work, *Tractatus Logico-Philosophicus* (1921), contended that philosophy should be primarily a "critique of language," or, "the logical clarification of thoughts." To him, the consideration of *ultimate* questions is irrelevant and meaningless. Since a person cannot speak of God in logical terms or in a way that can be proved by the senses, he should be silent.

But a Positive Attitude, Also

The first positive attitude toward the Bible began with the same Wittgenstein who had earlier affirmed the meaninglessness of religious language. This new development began with his later work, *Philosophical Investigations,* published after his death in 1951. In this work, the shift of emphasis was from the *meaning* of words to their *function.* In this later emphasis, the British philosopher affirmed that the situation, or context, is important because one understands the meaning of words only if one can locate them in the situation. The situation he calls a "language game." Thus religious language is a unique language. It cannot be thrown under the "game rules" of any other "language game" and be fairly judged. This means that the criteria for finding the adequacy of biblical and religious language must take into account unique purpose and function.

In the biblical language controversy, a pioneer on the positive side is Ian T. Ramsey. As a professor at Oxford University in England, Ramsey lives and works in the center of linguistic analysis study. He has made use of a work published in the eighteenth century, Butler's *Analogy of Religion,* which was directed against early empiricism. From Butler, Ramsey draws two categories, which he calls *discernment* and *commitment.* For Ramsey, these two categories are basic to religion.

Discernment

To bring *discernment* is an important part of the Bible's purpose. Ramsey seeks to illustrate discernment situations by calling forth various examples from life experience. For example, at certain times a situation becomes alive and personal to the degree that it discloses something hitherto unseen. Picture a cold courtroom. Here is a judge who usually employs legal, technical, and impersonal language. Before him is brought an old college friend. The impersonal situation suddenly becomes alive. The "light dawns," and there is discernment.

Commitment

The Bible also calls for *commitment.* Important discernments, vivid arousements, and crises call for the response of total commitment. However, total commitment, without any discernment whatever, would be bigotry and idolatry. On the other hand, to have the discernment without an appropriate commitment is the worst of all religious vices. Such would be insincerity and hypocrisy.

In order to fulfill its purposes of discernment and commitment, according to Ramsey, the Bible uses language in a peculiar or odd way. Metaphors are used in profusion. The biblical language is an object language which has been given special qualifications so that it is logically peculiar.

Taking words from common speech, a disclosure situation uses words for an uncommon purpose. When the oddness accomplishes it purposes, here is an opening of the eyes, a sense of "Aha, I get it!" Or, as Ramsey likes to put it, "The penny drops; the light dawns."

Casserly's Contribution

J. V. Langmead Casserly is in the forefront in establishing that God is a "*singular*" who reveals Himself in events as well as in words. This means that *event symbols* are especially important in talking about God. Certain events in the Bible are pointed out to be self-revelatory acts of the living God. In these cases, the *event symbols* do not portray something universal in the human condition; instead, they portray something specific and proper to the divine or singular existence.

In order to illustrate an event symbol, Casserly discusses the doctrine of the virgin birth. If the story of the virgin birth were meant to be a universal "myth," the obvious meaning would be that there is a radical incompatibility between sexuality and spirituality. Casserly rejects this Manichaean interpretation and affirms that the virgin birth narrative is not a myth symbol. On the contrary, it is an event symbol with a quite specific reference of an utterly singular character. If the virgin birth is considered as an event symbol, it means that the Son of God "enters into" the world process and does not "emerge out" of it. It is an entirely novel act of God, similar to the creation of the world. For Casserly, it is only as an event symbol that the virgin birth is capable of bearing a Christian meaning.

The distinction between myth symbols and event symbols is even clearer in connection with the resurrection narrative. For Casserly, the apostolic witness to the resurrection is not primarily a truth of faith. A Christian does not believe in the resurrection event because he has Christian faith. Actually, the opposite is true—a person has Christian faith because he believes in the resurrection event. The New Testament testimony to the resurrection is not a faith truth; it is a historical truth. This historical truth is that which arouses (or even causes) faith in the minds of those people who find themselves confronted by it. For Casserly, historical truth precedes faith in logic and in time. Faith is a trust in God, by whom the event was initiated and of whom it is a sign. In this light, the resurrection narrative is seen to be an event symbol which reveals the one living God in action and not a myth symbol which suggests a generality. If an event symbol is translated into a myth symbol, the meaning is altered.

For Casserly, religion was made by man, and it is therefore mythic. On the other hand, God gave the gospel, which is therefore eventual, or historic. In many cases, myth is existential and insightful; but only events are theologically revealing. Only from the event can be derived any knowledge of the God who is and acts. This is the living God who presents himself to men in the biblical testimony.

Biblical Language Is Unique

It is noteworthy that William Albright, G. Ernest Wright, and others are now advocating that the biblical language is unique. Otto Piper, of Princeton Theological Seminary, elaborates on the theme of the unique nature of the biblical language. He finds this biblical language rooted, for the most part, in the Hebrew mind, which is descriptive and historical, in contrast to the Greek analytical and dialectical mind.

The very concreteness of biblical language enables the biblical man to apprehend the reality about which the Bible speaks. In contrast, the abstract terminology of Greek philosophy surrenders concreteness for a world of concepts. It must be remembered that the Bible, in its use of concrete language and images, never exhausts the object about which it is speaking with one image. It is impossible, therefore, to learn the full truth concerning a subject matter from one concrete image that describes it. This is the reason why Jesus (and, also, many biblical writers) used many parables and images to point to one truth. God is a father, a king, a lord, and a husband. The writers are free to use new images, but some prove more effective and thus are used more often. The description of God's work in earthly terms is made possible by manifestations of the divine purpose in the world. It also happens that the same image can have different meanings. The shepherd may be God, or he may be the one who smites the flock.

The primary purpose in studying the Bible, therefore, must be to gain an experience of the realities described in the Bible. The Bible as such is not a textbook of science and philosophy. Although the Bible is concrete, it must not be thought that it is inconsistent and vague. It prefers the freedom of imagery to the dead rule of scientific terminology.

Claude Tresmontant

Claude Tresmontant, a French thinker, suggests that the Bible contains an implicit world view. He seeks to construct, from this implicit metaphysic, an explicit view. It is well to remember that any literature which expresses a way of life and a viewpoint on reality implies a metaphysic or world view. The metaphysic may be incorrect or inconsistent, but it is there.

The biblical world view is not reasoned out in a treatise as the Greeks worked out their perspective or philosophy. The Hebrews did not deal with the timeless issues of being and becoming, of matter and form, and of definition and demonstrations. For a person accustomed to such a type of thinking, it is rather strange to be thrown into a book which talks about widows and orphans and about the corruption of judges and of affairs in the marketplace.

Despite its concreteness, the biblical world view does have a structure, Tresmontant contends. There is an organically related and coherent whole to the biblical approach to reality. According to Tresmontant, supported to some extent by Cherbonnier, there are three primary categories in the biblical world view: creation, incarnation, and history. The biblical concept of creation prevents either metaphysical dualism or metaphysical monism. The biblical metaphysic is also characterized by the incarnation. The incarnation implies a special type of biblical personalism in which personal relationships between man and God are meaningful. The incarnation also implies that the knowledge of universals is subordinate to the knowledge of persons. It further implies that, within certain limitations, anthropomorphisms of God are legitimate because God is conceived as a person.

The biblical world view is also characterized by a historical view of reality. In the historical view, the singular or particular is the focus as over against the universal. The logic of the singular is based on categories which are appropriate to unique historical events and to per-

sonality. The concept of time which moves toward fulfilment is also implied by the biblical concept of history.

In summary, Tresmontant defends the uniqueness of
biblical language and bases it on a unique world view
which is dependent upon the biblical categories of creation, incarnation, and history. To properly understand the
biblical language, a person must first understand the
biblical world view.

If the biblical language is seen in the context of the
biblical world view, it is recognized that it is not primarily poetic language or scientific empirical language.
The primary function of biblical language is that man
may know the truth concerning the things of God's revelation. These concepts—"know" and "the truth"—must
be understood within the biblical world view. A primary
function of biblical language is a knowledge function.
The biblical view of knowledge is knowledge of a person
and not just knowledge through sense experience and
logic. It should be noted that biblical language is not
primarily poetry because it has a strong referential function which distinguishes it from poetry. It refers to the
redemptive acts of God in history.

In the biblical vocabulary, the presupposition of the
existence of God is not questioned. But there is a valid
type of verification. It is not scientific verification in the
narrow sense, but an existential verification by confrontation with the Person. This is a verification which is consistent with the basic premises of the biblical faith.
Whether a person wishes to call this "empirical" with
John MacMurray is a matter of little consequence, if he
recognizes that experience is broader than sense experience.

The emphasis on the empirical-logical world view of

the biblical writers, and the unique categories of creation, incarnation, and history are significant for an understanding of the dynamic, concrete, and descriptive nature of biblical langage. Verification is possible, but it must be the kind of verification appropriate to the biblical world view.

Conflicts in the area of religious language and developments in logical positivism and linguistic analysis have helped in many ways to develop a proper understanding of the nature and purpose of religious and biblical language. This is one Christian fight over the Bible that may have served a useful purpose. The criticisms suggested by the movements have helped to stimulate a restudy of the nature and purpose of religious and biblical language. All language, including the scientific, has been seen to have some convictional qualities. Competent scholars, trained in linguistic analysis, have pointed out that religious and biblical languages are meaningful if restricted to their own unique purposes. As linguistic studies have developed, a narrow empiricism has been revealed as inadequate. Out of the debates concerning religious language have come helpful studies by competent scholars who make a strong case for metaphysical and religious reality. The biblical model has been re-examined and has been shown to have much relevance and power. Distinctive biblical categories are seen to shed light on human experience. The inadequacies of both an *extreme* biblical literalism and demythologizing have been exposed. The dominance of idealistic metaphysics has been broken.

A task in the immediate future is to mediate the results of the work of the significant men in the language field to the general public. In a time of reaction against the formal and abstract, the vivid, concrete, and dynamic language of the Bible and the comprehensive and coherent world view which it represents should find a reception if adequately presented.

Summary

This chapter may not have been your particular cup of tea. But ideas which to the general public may appear abstruse and solely within the province of scholars are often basic to shaping the thinking of a limited number of leaders who then influence larger groups. The nature of biblical language is obviously in such an area. As you can see, there is fruitful cause for all kinds of controversy growing out of the above.

CHAPTER NINE

Subjective Factors
Breed Battles

It is more and more recognized that the subjective factor is important in approaching the Bible. The way we interpret or use the Bible, for example, is always colored by means of knowledge or experiences which we already possess. Karl Barth and Rudolf Bultmann realized this early in the twentieth century. Bultmann astonished his New Testament colleagues by welcoming Karl Barth's theological commentary on Romans. He said it was helpful because it was a revolt against the sterile exegesis that said it could by historical means define the content of the Bible with scientific exactitude. He and Barth agreed that it is impossible for any interpreter of the Bible to be uninfluenced by his theological and philosophical convictions. Important also are psychological, sociological, economic, and political presuppositions.

Christians fight over the Bible because they have differing models for interpretation and oftentimes will not admit it. It would be helpful if frankness about preliminary understanding were brought out in the open.

Bultmann himself admits that the existential philosophy of Heidegger helped him clarify his self-understanding and approach to the Bible. He perhaps does not quite as readily admit that he is also a kind of historian who holds to an unbreakable chain of cause and effect in history. In the relationship between the historian and the philosopher, it becomes clear that "pre-understanding" and "pre-supposition" are related as a part to the whole. For Bultmann, history is a closed continuum which is limited to cause and effect relationships in a time-space framework. As a historian, Bultmann candidly rejects the biblical world view which he says is intolerable in the twentieth century. No intelligent and honest man can believe in a pre-existent deity who becomes incarnate by way of a virgin birth. Furthermore, he cannot believe in one who performs nature-miracles, who dies a substitutionary death, who rises bodily from the grave, who ascends to heaven, and who will return visibly to earth to judge the world and inaugurate the Kingdom of God. Neither can the modern historian believe in a God who acts directly in history.

Conservatives Disagree

In contrast, *conservatives* accept the fact that God did break through into history as the Bible records. God is not only active in history but he acts freely and purposely above and beyond history. This could be called a controlled continuum. God has established laws but is not a prisoner of his own laws. God is free to act as He does in the miracles and resurrection of Jesus.

Emil Fuchs, a disciple of Bultmann, has developed existential interpretation into a special theory of hermeneutics. Mastery and acceptance of existential philosophy is a prerequisite for engaging in fruitful exegesis according to this approach.

For Karl Barth, the claim to be a completely objective interpreter is a laughable delusion. Worry about his lack of objectivity, many nearly paralyze the interpreter and hinder him from hearing and responding to the Scripture with his whole being.

Barth, however, does not feel that the interpreter

should search out any congenial philosophy as a basis for understanding the Bible. There is to be no demythologizing. The whole of the Bible is to be heard. God Himself, through His world and Spirit, helps to create in man the right perspective.

Evangelical Scholars

Evangelical scholars find that Barth's emphases on God's grace in Christ has caused him to underplay God's holiness. Creation is even secondary to grace. This forces Barth to an allegorical interpretation of some of the Old Testament. Furthermore, his view of inspiration is weak compared to his doctrine of revelation.

In a later chapter, attention will be given to ancient and modern interpreters who were unduly influenced by Platonic philosophy. This influence undergirded an allegorical approach to the Bible, that continues to be popular among prominent interpreters.

The Rationalistic Era

In the eighteenth century, Deism and the Enlightenment set the stage for a rationalistic approach to the Bible. The religious values in the Bible were not to be found in any divine self-revelation break into history but only in the timeless truths contained in the Bible. These universal truths were determined by human reason. From this rationalistic perspective, miracles are simply impossible, neither could Jesus be the divine Son of God. A proper "historical" approach sought to penetrate behind Gospel portraits of Jesus as a divine being—to reconstruct a purely "historical" portrait. This ended up in a naturalistic, non-supernatural picture of Jesus of Nazareth.

This initial rationalistic approach to the Bible which inaugurated the historical method was modified in the nineteenth century under the influence of the idealistic philosophy of Hegel. Hegel interpreted history as the manifestation of absolute idea or spirit in human affairs and in the universe. Hegel's system involved a dialectical pattern of tension between one position (thesis) and a second position (antithesis), from whose interaction a third position (synthesis) emerged, bringing into being a new insight or aspect of reality.

Under the influence of the philosophy of Hegel, F. C. Baur abandoned the rationalistic effort to find timeless truths in the New Testament. Instead he found in the historical movements of the early church the unfolding of wisdom and spirit. Theological reflection began over the question of the place of the law in the church. The history of the apostolic age was interpreted in terms of the conflict over this question. Paul, the first Christian theologian, took the position that the Christian was freed from the law (thesis). Jewish Christianity, represented by James and Peter, took the opposite position that the law was binding upon Christians (antithesis). Out of the conflict between Pauline and Jewish Christianity emerged a synthesis in the church of the second century. This synthesis effected a successful harmonization of the two contradictory positions.

Books which clearly reflect either Pauline or Jewish theology were thought to be early. Books which reflected the synthesis were late. This critical principle led Baur to conclude that only four epistles were authentically Pauline.

A New Turn

A new turn in historical interpretation was made under the influence of the theology of Ritschl and men who were in his school. These men interpreted the essence of

Christianity as a pure spiritual-ethical religion, proclaimed by and embodied in the life and mission of Jesus.

Jesus was seen as a great religious personality who taught an ideal ethical religion, which had universal validity apart from its historical setting. After His death, Jesus' pure ethical religion was modified. He was deified and exalted, thus becoming the object of Christian faith and preaching.

This liberal interpretation, which saw Jesus as an ethical teacher of God's love rather than an incarnate Saviour was important in the fundamentalist-modernist controversy in America in the 1920s and 1930s. The scientific scholars were the ones who said they had found the historical Jesus in the ethical prophet. The idea of the divine incarnate Saviour was identified with outmoded pre-scientific supernaturalism.

Machen and many another conservative scholar has been vindicated. Long ago they pointed out that the old liberal Jesus was the construction of German idealistic theology. It is now recognized that this liberal Jesus never existed except as a reconstruction in the mind of the liberal critic.

The next development of this non-objective historical method resulted from the influence of evolutionary philosophy. This philosophy was applied to Biblical history and gave rise to comparative religions method. The underlying assumption of this approach is that the religion of both Israel and the early church is an evolutionary development. The Bible is not seen as a book of theology, but as a record of religious experience.

Albert Schweitzer

Out of this background came Albert Schweitzer with his thesis that Jesus was a Jew with a single message which was that the end of the world was imminent. Schweitzer was influenced by the researchers who were pointing out the importance in Judaism of apocalyptic writings such as Enoch and the Apocalypse of Baruch. Schweitzer held that this apocalyptic coming of God's Kingdom was Jesus' only concern. According to Schweitzer, Jesus died in disillusionment. Historically, Jesus belongs to first-century Judaism and has no relevance for the modern man.

Paul was interpreted by the comparative religion school in terms of Hellenistic religions, then prevalent in the Graeco-Roman world. The center of Paul's belief was said to have been the heavenly Lord patterned after the pagan cults, and Pauline sacraments, baptism and the Lord's Supper were understood as adaptations of the cultic rites of the mystery religions.

Bultmann, already referred to, was a product of the history-religion school. He combined this school with another philosophical presupposition, that of existentialism, which we have already noted.

It has been very disconcerting for evangelicals that the continued theological assumption of the history of religion school is that there is no room for the immediate acting of God in history. In other words, the supernatural must be dispensed with. For this reason, many evangelicals have felt that biblical criticism as it has developed has been an enemy of sound evangelical faith.

In recent years, a more sensitive approach has been developed by men like Oscar Cullmann. Revelation and redemption are seen to occur in historical events, culminating in the event of Jesus Christ. These redemptive events are always accompanied by a word of interpretation. The interpretation belongs itself to redemptive history. In the New Testament, the word of interpretation stems from eyewitnesses, particularly the apostles and prophets. The rise of the New Testament canon marks the final term of the entire preceding history of interpretation. This means that the New Testament history must be interpreted theologically.

It has been seen that each interpreter has a conscious or unconscious model for biblical interpretation.

Luther found this touchstone in the Pauline concept of justification by faith, especially as it is given by Romans and Galatians. The book of James has little of this emphasis and was called by Luther a book of straw. It is obvious that Luther over-emphasized the theme of justification by faith because of his struggle against medieval Roman Catholic legalism.

In the nineteenth century the Pauline concept of "in Christ" was thought by many to be the key to Paul's thinking. This divergence from the Reformation view has led in recent years to a reopening of the problem of that which is the central interpretive key of the Bible. Scholars have turned again to ask the Bible itself to disclose its own theological center.

It is generally agreed that Luther had a valid insight in seeking an interpretative touchstone when he started with Paul. It is held now by many scholars, however, that the doctrine of "justification by faith" and the concept "in Christ" are both inadequate and lack comprehensiveness.

It would be a mistake, however, to consider the "in Christ" and the "justification by faith" principles in Paul and in the New Testament as two more or less conflicting points of view. It is not right to present the dilemma in such a way that either the "in Christ" or the "justification by faith" keys would secure the actual entrance to Paul and the New Testament. The doctrine of "justification by faith" and the concept "in Christ" are both inadequate and lack enough comprehension. For example, the concept "in

Christ" is part of a wider scheme. It needs to be balanced by "in Adam."

Here we begin to get the clue to the understanding of Paul and the New Testament. It is Paul's scheme of "holy history," or "salvation history," or "redemptive history," which brackets together both his theory and his practice, both his labors and his writings, both his missionary work and his theological thinking. Here in "holy history," or "redemptive history," affirms Reginald Fuller, we have the real key to Paul's life and thought. The Dutch scholar Ridderbos likewise contends that the term "redemptive-historical"—which is his translation of the German expression *Heilsgeschichtlich*—expresses a new and broader outlook. "What Paul sets before us may be described as *Heilsgeschichte*. I know of no satisfactory rendering of this German word, and prefer, therefore, to allow it to stand. 'Redemptive history' suggests that history redeems, and 'history of salvation' suggests that salvation is an institution." Here is a partial statement of a concept which is helping some of our most fruitful and competent biblical scholars to make sense of many of the most difficult parts of the New Testament and the Bible as a whole. In fact, this "redemptive-historical" perspective embraces both the concept of "justification by faith" and "in Christ."

Other competent biblical scholars add a further qualifying word to the term "holy history." This word is "eschatological." Since the days when Albert Schweitzer pointed out that eschatology is the dominant motif of the Bible, no competent biblical scholar has been able to eliminate the centrality of eschatology in his study. There is an eschatological orientation which pervades the New Testament. The Old Testament is the inspired record of the divine activity in history in which God initiated and carried forward His purposes for man's salvation. The purposes of God have been and are being accomplished in history, past and present. And yet the great purpose of God is future. In the New Testament, a different orientation is found. The element of expectation and hope remains and is still dominant. The full experience of the realities of redemption and salvation remain for the future. However, salvation is no longer merely an object of future hope. In the totality of the Christ-event are birth, life, teachings, death, resurrection, and ascension. God has entered into human history to bring certain salvation realities by virtue of which the blessings of the future eschatological salvation have become objects of present experience.

The New Testament describes the entire sweep of human existence in terms of "this age" and "the age to come." In the first coming of Christ the blessings of the future age have been made available in the spiritual realm for human enjoyment. However, the evil age continues and the uniform biblical testimony is that the fullness of redemptive blessings awaits the glorious appearing of "the age to come." The main emphasis of the Bible is that the age to come is always an object of hope and of expectation. The present age continues to be evil because Satan is still its god and will be until the *parousia* of Christ. While the boundary between the two ages is still future and eschatological, the age to come has reached back into the present so that in a sense the present age and the future age run side by side (1 Cor. 10:11). Biblical thought is through and through eschatological. The salvation themes which have already been accomplished attain their depth and significance because they are a partial but real anticipation of the future. The future eschatological consummation is entirely indispensable, because, without it, the present salvation blessings will ever be incomplete.

It would seem that the most fruitful way in which to state the key to interpreting the Bible would be in terms of a combination of the eschatological emphasis and the "holy history" emphasis. We will, therefore, coin the phrase "eschatological-holy history" and suggest that it is the key to interpreting and understanding the Bible.

Since "eschatological-holy history" traces the divine acts in redemptive history, the interpreter must expect progression in the revelation. The various stages of prophetic interpretation of redemptive history are equally inspired and authoritative, but they embody differing degrees of apprehension of the meanings involved. The Old Testament interpretation of the divine redemption furnishes only broad outlines of the consummation of God's ultimate purpose. This perspective from which God granted the prophets to see the great redemptive events is that of their own environment—the history of the nation Israel.

The gospel proclaimed by Jesus and the gospel proclaimed by Paul are not different gospels. Any seeming differences are due to the different points of *perspective* along the holy line of redemptive history. For example, Christ could hardly instruct his disciples in the fullness of the gracious and redeeming significance of his death. He had a difficult time in conveying to them that His messianic death was to be a fact in the divine purpose (Matt. 16:21-23). The apostles who couched their writings in different terms were raised up after the event of the messianic death and resurrection had become a part of redemptive history. One of the first men to point out the importance of interpreting a particular passage according to its place in the divine-redemptive line was the great German scholar Von Hofmann.

The public ministry of Jesus.—Failure to understand

"eschatological-holy history" as the key to interpreting the Bible has caused great confusion among theologians in their endeavor to describe how much of the kingdom or to what extent the kingdom had come in Jesus' public ministry. C. H. Dodd and many following after him have tended to concentrate attention on Mark 1:15 and Matthew 9:37ff. and say that with the ministry of Jesus the kingdom was realized. Perhaps a better way of putting it from the perspective of "eschatological-holy history" is not that God had acted finally and conclusively in a realized way in Christ's public ministry but that He was in the process of acting. The kingdom of God had started its work among the Pharisees by virtue of his deeds and work during his earthly ministry (Luke 19:20ff.). He talked of the future when He would die on the cross as a ransom for many and take life again in resurrection. This was to be an even more decisive and greater coming of the kingdom. He finally described the day when the Son of man would come in glory to bring his kingdom to victory (Matt. 25:31ff.). The kingdom among men began with the activity of Christ in his public ministry, but its fullness would only come in the end.

The parables of Jesus.—The parables illustrate the mystery of the kingdom. The concept of mystery has an Old Testament background in the book of Daniel, where it involves the disclosure of divine secrets to men. In the New Testament, mystery is a disclosed secret, the revelation of the divine purpose. It was no secret that God would one day establish his kingdom in glory and apocalyptic power—this was orthodox Jewish theology. The mystery is that the kingdom which is to come finally in apocalyptic power, as foreseen in Daniel, has, in fact, entered into the world in advance in a secret form to work quietly within the lives of men. This is a mystery, a new revelation. The Old Testament gave no such promise. The kingdom the Jews expected was a display of divine power that would overthrow Rome. This was why the people were so stirred up by the announcement of John the Baptist and then by Jesus, that the kingdom of God has come near.

Each of the parables in Matthew 13 illustrates the mystery of the kingdom, that the kingdom of God, which is yet to come in power and great glory, is actually present among men in advance in an unexpected form to bring to men in the present evil age the blessings of the age to come.

The parable of the mustard seed illustrates the truth that the kingdom, which one day will be a great tree, is already present in the world in a tiny insignificant form. A mustard seed is not a suitable illustration of the gradual growth which is often seen in the parable, for it was a relatively quick-growing plant. The Jews could not understand how one could talk about the coming of the kingdom apart from such a glorious and mighty manifestation of God's rule in some outward demonstration. How could this coming glorious kingdom, which would shelter the multitudes of the righteous, have anything to do with a movement so insignificant as that of Jesus and His disciples? Jesus answered: First a tiny seed, later a large tree. The future form of the kingdom is not to be measured by its initial insignificance.

This, then, is the mystery of the kingdom. It comes quietly, humbly, without fire from heaven, without a blaze of glory, without a rending of the mountain or a cleaving of the skies. It can be rejected by hard hearts; it can be choked out; its life may sometimes seem to wither and die. But it is the kingdom of God. It brings the miracle of a divine life among men. It introduces them into the blessings of the divine rule. It is to them the supernatural work of God's grace. And, this same kingdom, this same supernatural power of God, will yet manifest itself at the end of the age, this time not quietly within the lives of those who received it, but in power and great glory, purging all sin and evil from the earth. Such is the gospel of the kingdom.

Thus, we have attempted to give examples of how the "eschatological-holy history" key throws light on difficult and controversial verses and passages in the New Testament. In attempting to set forth a viewpoint, undoubtedly an overemphasis has been made in certain places. Even though the "eschatological-holy history" approach is different from that which many have been accustomed to use, it is still the central task of biblical scholarship to seek that which is the guiding key. Many competent men feel that the "eschatological-holy history" viewpoint is the key which is most in keeping with the central emphasis of the New Testament.

This "eschatological-holy history" orientation properly understood, is not just other-worldly and escapist. It is related to life here and now. Our hope for the future is really a fulfillment and completion of the gains, experiences, and labors of this age. The biblical world view, properly understood, does not encourage asceticism or dualism. Even nature is to share in the renewed creation. Such a view of nature constitutes a proper background for science. The biblical view of hope affirms the reality and meaning of history and time without falling into the delusion of Communism which is that time and history can fulfill themselves. Biblical hope gives depth to life.

We need to recover the biblical dynamic and perspective. It would give us courage and freedom which are desperately needed. G. Beasley-Murray of Spurgeon's

College points out that biblical hope including the second coming of Christ undergirds an intense present. This hope gives an incentive to action. It gives the Christian a prophetic freedom which enables him to be more firm and decisive in regard to ethical matters. It gives the Christian a personal dynamic. This expectant attitude also gives a solid sense of responsibility. The coming one is the lord and judge to whom we must be prepared to give an account of the stewardship of our time and influence and talents.

CHAPTER TEN

They Differ
Over World Views

Christians fight over the Bible because they differ over the continuing validity of the biblical description of the world and of man.

Liberals contend that the biblical authors shared a world view that did not make a sharp distinction between the natural and the supernatural. The people in the early centuries tended to enlarge and magnify events. They lived in a prescientific age and had little sense of causality. In fact, enlarging events into miracles and myths helped people to believe. It was a credulous age.

Today, however, myths about Christ coming on clouds of glory and other similar biblical stories, according to the liberals, detract from the spiritual meaning of Christianity. It is important, therefore, to eliminate the outer mythical framework and to keep the inner meaning of biblical events. The inner meaning can help people to attain self-understanding.

The factual content or historicity of biblical stories has little significance for the liberal mind. The question of whether or not "it really happened" is secondary to the question of its help for human existence today. Rudolf Bultmann is a well-known exponent of this view. The emphasis of this approach is to retain the "preaching" about man's self-understanding but dispense with the "myth."

Neo-Evangelicals will accept the fact that the biblical

language in regard to external things is popular and pre-scientific. It is not anti-scientific. E. J. Carnell calls the biblical language concerning natural things, "optical language." It is a language of appearance—the Bible describes the visible form of the world. As Calvin suggested, Moses was not interested in giving us technical astronomy. He was interested in us and our redemption rather than the stars. Moses spoke in popular style. Calvin further suggested that God purposely accommodated himself and allowed the prophets and apostles to speak through normal patterns of speech in relation to natural phenomena.

This external framework of life, which is constantly changing, is called a "world picture." Science has freedom to work in this area.

However, for "God-man" and "man-man" relations (sin and salvation) and consummation, the biblical material is perennially valid. This theological material describes the beginning, purpose, and end of the life of man and history. According to Eric Rust, this world view fulfills certain criteria it sets for itself. These criteria are: man's restoration to God through Jesus Christ; and guidance for the Christian life.

Modern science cannot and has no right to challenge these revealed truths and categories. They are bound up with the relation of God to the world. Science is concerned to describe the processes of the natural order or proximate causes. It cannot deal with creation and preservation.

Bible interpreters should not allow alien world views to destroy the revealed biblical world view. The Christian world view is divinely inspired and infallible for faith and practice.

The biblical world view is built around the historical

actuality of saving events. Oftentimes accompanying God's self-revelation in biblical times were unique signs such as the burning bush. If Jesus did not objectively die on the cross and rise again, the statements that "Jesus died for our sins" and "rose that we might be raised" are meaningless. Furthermore, these events are confirmed in countless changed lives and personal experience.

As already indicated, according to Calvin, God gave objective visions to the prophets and apostles. These are important for giving substance to the Christian faith. New methods of communication are to be used that are helpful only in the long run if the revealed world view is proclaimed.

CHAPTER ELEVEN

How Does One
Interpret the Bible?

No area is more fruitful for Christian conflict than that of biblical interpretation. Differing emphases on the principles of biblical interpretation probably do more to separate the various Christian groups than any other single matter. The reason is not difficult to understand. Because of the importance of the Bible as the word of God, knowing what the Bible says is obviously of prime importance.

How does one go about it? The puzzled layman might ask: "Well, why don't you just read the Bible and see what it says?" It seems all so simple.

Scholars demur.

They explain their positions to each other, but they do have a bit of difficulty with that layman. Let us see why.

Pre-understanding

It was Bultmann who saw clearly that there is no such thing as a neutral interpretation of the Bible. This recognition of the framework of thought utilized by each interpreter is called "pre-understanding." This conscious or unconscious framework influences the way principles of biblical interpretation are utilized by people in the mainstream of historic Christianity as well as by groups who interpret the Bible but are called cultic. Here is another area where Christians and cultic groups fight over the Bible.

Many Christians, as well as cultic groups such as Christian Science and Unity, have used what is called the allegorical method of interpretation.

Allegory teaches that beneath the ordinary and obvious meaning of a passage is the real or spiritual meaning. The chief goal of the allegorical interpreter is to seek to decipher these so-called spiritual and hidden meanings.

This system of interpretation was first developed by the Greeks as early as 520 B.C. for the interpretation of Homer and Hesiod. It was later utilized by Jewish interpreters such as Aristobulus (second century B.C.) and Philo of Alexandria (first century A.D.). The method was then adopted by most of the Christian interpreters and dominated exegesis until the Protestant Reformation.

If it had not been for the authority of the dogmas of the medieval church, interpretation would have been complete chaos in the Middle Ages. There was little concern for historical background. The Bible was treated as a one-level collection, to be expounded without regard to historical background. There was a general ignorance of the biblical languages.

Bible verses were said to have two, three, and four meanings. Mickelsen points out that "Jerusalem," for the medieval interpreters, could have reference to the literal city in Palestine. Allegorically, it could mean the church. Morally, it could refer to the human soul. From a future perspective, "Jerusalem" refers to the heavenly city. The word "sea" could mean a gathering of water, the Bible, the present age, the human heart, the active life, heathen, or baptism. The historical interpretaion (the plain, evident meaning) was described as "milk" while the spiritual interpretations were described as exhilarating "wine."

A favorite book in the Middle Ages was the Song of Songs. The Bible was made to mean what it plainly did not say. It became a magician's bag from which interpreters drew forth mysteries and truths to decorate their own imaginative worlds. In one age Moses and the Apostles were made to speak as if they were Plato. In another age they spoke as if they were Aristotle. This pursuit of multiple meanings is really a magical approach to language and literary works. It removes any certainty of meaning.

The search for hidden meanings became so extreme that a premium was placed on the unusual and the surprising. Augustine, in the fifth century A.D., found interpretations fruitful in proportion to their unusual or difficult nature. For example, the ark is the figure of the church which is rescued by the wood on which Christ hung. Its very dimensions represent the human body in which Christ came. The door in the side signifies the wounds in the side of the crucified Christ.

In more modern times, men like Emanuel Swedenborg of Sweden and groups like Unity and Christian Science have utilized allegorical interpretation. In both Unity and Christian Science, grammar, context, and history are ignored. The important meanings are the hidden or spiritual meanings.

In Christian Science, Mrs. Eddy claims to have discovered the allegorical key to interpretation. The standard dictionary meanings of words are not sufficient. A spiritual glossary must be provided. From the glossary it is learned that Canaan is sensuous belief. Dan is animal magnetism. Sheep stands for innocence. Eden is the mortal, material body. Fowls stand for aspiration. Genesis One is not a story of the creation of the world but a description of the spiritual world.

It is obvious that when the grammatical-historical approach is abandoned, there is no way to control exegesis.

In reaction to allegory, other Christian groups, as well as cultic representatives such as Jehovah's Witnesses, have used the extreme literal approach.

The founder of the Jewish "hyperliteralist" emphasis in interpretation is generally considered to be Ezra. In the Babylonian captivity, the Scriptures took on more importance, and scribal interpreters became more influential. Some sound principles of interpretation were developed by rabbinical interpreters such as Hillel and Eliezar. An unfortunate emphasis on "letterism" or hyperliteralism, however, developed among the majority of Jewish interpreters. In their devotion to the details of the text, such as phrases, clauses, and single words, they missed the essential meaning of the passage. Later they combined this hyperliteralism with allegory and tradition and developed many grotesque interpretations. They bogged down in the trivialities and the incidental. In the period after the Reformation, seventeenth century Protestants tended to idolize the Bible to such an extent as to miss its essential meaning. The Bible was not seen as an historical and literary book but simply as dogma. In more recent times, Jehovah's Witnesses, other cultic groups, and Fundamentalists have tended toward hyperliteralism. Grammar, historical and literary content, and central biblical motifs are largely ignored.

Jehovah's Witnesses

Few other groups make as extensive use of Scripture in their message as do the Jehovah's Witnesses. They parade as Bible students. Almost 75% of their literature is composed of Bible quotations. They say that only false interpretations were given in the past, and that Russell and

Rutherford have given us the proper interpretations. The Bible without their interpretation is of no more value than any ordinary history book. They maintain that their own translation is more accurate than the others. But actually their New World translation is inadequate and slanted toward their views. John 1:1 says, "The word was *a* God." They say that prophecy is in a large part detailed prediction. Christ began his secret second coming in 1914. The biblical apocalyptic literature dealing with last things in symbolic language is the most important and normative. Ezekiel and Daniel are of particular emphasis. It is to be taken in a literal and mathematical sense. In summary, you might say that they can more accurately be considered a mutation or odd type of conservative apocalyptic Judaism, rather than a type of Christianity. It is literalism run mad. It is an unscriptural juggling with days and dates.

Hermeneutics

Among Christian groups in the more normative Christian tradition, a convenient and widely used approach is called hermeneutics. Interpretation or exegesis is the actual explanation of the text utilizing the principles or theory. There are numerous ways in which the generally accepted and basic principles of biblical interpretation could be presented. One convenient and widely used approach is to consider the principles under the designations of grammatical, historical, theological, and practical. Some will suggest variations of arrangement, wording and order but the principles will be essentially the same. They are sometimes called the grammatical-historical-theological principles.

The advantages of utilizing these principles are many. This approach exercises some control over interpretation.

A check is placed on the temptation of interpreters to seek out hidden meanings in the Bible. Furthermore, the grammatical-historical-theological approach has proved itself through the years. Scholars and laymen who follow these principles have made constructive and abiding contributions to Bible knowledge and understanding.

Syntax

Disagreement arises when these principles are neglected or improperly used. When correct syntax or the relation of words is ignored, a doctrinal heresy may arise. In John 1:1 it is affirmed that, "The Word was God." The word "God" is a predicate nominative in the Greek language. As such this phrase cannot be translated, "God was the Word." The syntax will not allow this translation. Theologically, the latter translation, which is not allowable, would not leave any room for God outside of the Word.

Good translations and commentaries make much of the delicate meanings of verbs, nouns, and clauses and their relationships. The verb is especially important in Greek. In Hebrew the verb system is less complex but important nevertheless.

Thought Method

Misunderstandings of Scripture arise when the method of thought of the Biblical writer is ignored. The biblical writers wrote for the men of their own times and used the forms of thought of the men of the times. An interpreter must seek to understand the method of reasoning of the biblical author. The people of the Bible lived in a thought world that was more accustomed to paradox than precision. They expressed themselves in ways which cannot be forced into the rigid and exact categories of modern

Western thought and logic. Traditional interpretations may need revising in the light of present knowledge of Hebrew ways of thinking and speaking. Stibbs points out that the phrase, "I loved Jacob and I hated Esau" (Mal. 1:2,3), is the way the Hebrew states a comparison rather than a direct opposite. It might better be translated, "I loved Jacob more than Esau."

Poetic Passages

Who has not heard of misunderstandings and even doctrinal conflicts concerning poetic passages in the Bible. Each type of literature in the Bible should be understood in the light of its own literary type. In straightforward narrative, words are taken at face value. In poetic sections, a different approach is needed. Fortunately, the RSV and certain other modern translations indicate in the printing which is the formally poetic.

Jesus said, "If your right eye causes you to sin, pluck it out" (Matt. 5:20). Is he suggesting self-mutilation? Obviously this verse must not be interpreted in a literalistic way. As Mounce has emphasized, Jesus often used hyperbole and figurative language to stress truth. Herod was called "the fox" (Luke 13:32). Paul referred to James and Cephas as "pillars in the Jerusalem church" (Gal. 2:9). The word "pillar" must not be taken to refer to a shaft of masonry work. The literary context makes clear its meaning. Peter describes the devil as a roaring lion (Peter 5:8). Metaphoric language must be recognized as such.

The statement, "Let us make man in our image, after our likeness" (Gen. 1:26), is not to be taken as describing different parts of man. Some of the early church fathers taught that image and likeness in this verse referred to different aspects of man. If an interpreter understands

Hebrew parallelism, he will see that both image and likeness have exactly the same meaning. The repetition is for emphasis.

Context Ignored

Doctrinal conflicts also arise because people ignore context. Basic to any understanding of a word or verse in the Bible is the context—both immediate and general. For a farmer, a donkey means a beast of burden. In the context of a national election in the United States, it means the Democratic Party.

If verses are seen in context, states Mounce, difficulties in interpretation have a way of solving themselves. The "work out your own salvation" phrase of Philippians 2:12 makes sense if seen in context. It is a call to concern for the welfare of others as God's design for the deliverance of the Philippian church from a threatening disunity (cf. Philippians 2:1–5; 4:2–3).

Lorenzo Dow ignored context in seeking to find a text against top-knot hair styles in his time. His famous sermon "Top Knot, Come Down" found its text in Matthew 24:17: "Let him which is on the housetop not come down." The book of James and the book of Romans are sometimes said to contradict each other. Seen in context, however, the larger purpose of the writers was different in each case. Instead of contradicting each other, they actually complement each other.

The Historical Principle

Many so-called "Spiritual" or "Pietistic" groups neglect the second basic principle of biblical exegesis which is usually called the historical principle. Since the mid-nineteenth century this principle has been a basic premise of all serious interpreters. It includes a consideration of the geographical (spatial background), historical (temporal background), and cultural (material and social background) materials.

Since the Bible originated in a historical context, it is obvious that it can only be understood in an accurate and complete way if this historical background is studied. An interpreter must seek to creep out of his twentieth century skin and identify himself with the feelings and life of the biblical times.

Avoid Overshadowing

The more critical—or *liberal*—interpreters oftentimes allow the historical background and culture to overshadow the actual content being considered. For an *evangelical* interpreter, the biblical writers are considered to be men of their times and yet men above their times. The more rationalistic interpreter would tend to place less emphasis on the content and give more attention to the reconstruction of the original setting. For both, however, the historical background is important. The dimensions of time and history are essential to understanding the New Testament in its own terms.

With women's liberation in the forefront, either the neglect or overemphasis on historical background will cause a distortion of relevant biblical passages. For example, according to 1 Corinthians 11:5, the women of Corinth were to keep their heads veiled when they prayed. Cartledge suggests that the historical context helps to illuminate this statement. In ancient Corinth, pure women wore their veils in public. Some of the Corinthian Christian women decided to throw off that restriction. Paul protested for he did not want the Christian women to be mistaken for the sacred prostitutes of the Aphrodite cult of Corinth.

An enforcement of veiling today on the basis of a biblical command would obviously ignore the historical context. Fortunately, there is ample material available today to study history and culture. The interpreter should avail himself of Bible histories, atlases, and studies of the biblical people and cultures.

An adequate and balanced study of historical background should help to reduce conflicts between Christian groups. In order to communicate any message from one culture to another, Mickelsen suggests that it is necessary to understand both of the cultures involved. It is likewise important not to change the message while communicating it. This involves a rigorous study of the context of the particular biblical era involved, the modern cultural context of the interpreter, and the modern cultural background of his hearers. To know and to study the historical and cultural context is now recognized as basic to sound interpretation and communication.

Recognized, yes—but Christians still fight over issues that arise from this!

As indicated above, *Evangelicals* in the 1920s and '30s reacted to an over-emphasis on the grammatical, critical, and historical principles on the part of some interpreters. The historical critics succeeded in textual work, grammar, literary history, and archaeology, but they often missed the theological meaning of the Bible. A great assortment of facts and data was analyzed and classified. The interest of the trained interpreter was oftentimes focused on historical reconstruction. The meaning or frame of reference, however, was lacking. The theological and practical principles were largely ignored. Since World War I, biblical interpretation has refashioned itself in significant theological circles in a way which places more emphasis on the theological and practical principles of biblical interpretation. Commentaries emphasize the underlying structural unity of the Bible. In much current exegetical work, the interpreters are once again seeking to be obedient to the nature of the Bible. The historical question and the theological question are both asked in approaching the Bible. What happened in the Bible and the interpretation of the happenings are being seen as one inseparable event.

The Theological Principle

And so the third basic principle is the *theological principle*. As has been indicated above, interpretation of the Bible is an attempt to discover and describe the meaning of the biblical books. It can be scientific only when it takes seriously the testimony of the biblical writers. The interpreter is not to bring his own ideas to the Bible. The theological themes confront the interpreter in the material and his method must recognize their presence. The Bible is only incidentally language and history. It was not written just for historical or esthetic ends. Essentially it was written as a book of faith. The primary conviction of the Bible writers is that a gracious God has acted in history in order to create in Christ a people for himself. Interpretation must seek to understand these theological insights. It must be obedient to the nature of the Bible. To do this sound interpretation must be both historical and theological. Fortunately, since World War II, new tools such as theological word books have been produced. These studies indicate, for example, that Jesus was not simply a refined teacher of the Golden Rule and the general fatherhood of God. Rather he was accepted as the Messiah who fulfilled in his life, death, and resurrection the promises of the Old Testament prophets that God in the fulness of time would act redemptively in history. The biblical reports do not record objective external events presented in terms satisfactory to the classification methods of natural sciences. The writers and reporters were involved in the events and both remembered and interpreted. What happened and the theological interpretation are fused together. The writers were confronted by, overwhelmed by, and found new existence in their encounter with God in Jesus Christ. Jesus is described in the Bible by men who believed in Him as the Messiah. The escape of the Hebrews across the Red Sea is reported by men who remembered, were caught up in the deliverance, and saw it as God's action.

In many cases there is an interval between the biblical events and the literary fixation of the witness. As Mays has pointed out, the Bible is the result of a complex process of forming, shaping, and growth. This interval of time between events and text is not neutral and vacant. As the events were told and retold, they gained a new dynamic contemporaneity. The witnesses themselves confirmed and deepened their understanding and insight concerning the original event.

Evangelicals

Evangelicals are in conflict with those interpreters who believe the Bible can be adequately understood or interpreted apart from a personal relationship to the God of the Bible. The interpreter is not like an experimenter in natural sciences. He has presuppositions of which he should be aware. These presuppositions should always be subject to the testing of confrontation with the Bible. Of course, all men have presuppositions in any type of thinking or interpreting. At least the Christian interpreter admits his biases and prejudices. The Bible cannot be fully understood from the outside by grammar, logic, rhetoric, and history alone. It must be understood from its center. The Bible's center yields itself best to men who have a personal relation with God through Jesus Christ and who are indwelt by the Spirit of God. The pietistic school has probably put too much emphasis on the experiential aspect of interpretation. On the other hand, it is possible for a rationalistic interpreter to miss the theological heart of the Bible with his exclusive emphasis on the grammar and the historical background.

Proof-texting Creates Conflict

As has been noted, a common practice among Christians is to engage in an arbitrary selection of Bible texts to undergird an ethical view or doctrine when convenient. Other texts equally important but inconvenient to the view or result desired, are passed over, played down, or artificially harmonized. Slavery, for example, was defended on biblical grounds as divinely ordained, or at least permissible.

Proof-texting of this sort, as well as allegorizing, was widely practiced in the Middle Ages. To counteract this approach, the Protestant Reformers in the sixteenth century developed the "analogy of faith" principle of interpretation.

Several emphases listed below are included under this emphasis. When these emphases are neglected, unnecessary conflicts arise.

The New Testament is the norm for interpreting the Old Testament. Prophecy is not self-interpretive but should follow New Testament insights. This does not mean that the New Testament rejects the Old Testament. Instead, the New Testament fulfills the Old Testament.

The Bible is to be understood from its center—its heart —its Christ. This principle includes doctrinal interpretation. This means that difficult verses or verses on the periphery must be understood in the light of the plainest passages. The Bible is mistreated when it is said to be primarily a handbook of prophecy and world politics or hyper-dispensationalism. The main burden of our theology should rest on the teaching of the New Testament. The Old Testament is the economy or book of preparation and the New Testament is the economy or book of fulfilment. Protestants argue that Seventh Day Adventism is cultic when it converts an Old Testament emphasis on the seventh day into a New Testament principle. Evangelicals would contend that Roman Catholicism is cultic when it rests its distinctives such as prayers for the dead on the Old Testament Apocrypha. Even Jerome said the Apocrypha were good for edification but not for doctrine.

Systematic Passages

Systematic passages should have priority over incidental passages. For example, justification is treated in a systematic teaching form in Romans and Galatians. According to Carnell, these books should be the primary guides for discussion of this doctrine. Incidental and ambiguous verses should be subordinated or looked at in the light of the larger and clearer emphases. This approach is actually the kind of procedure which educated people follow when any body of material or system of thought is under examination. Universal principles are to be sought in the midst of local ceremonies. It was through foot washing that Jesus Christ taught the principle of love and humility. Paul's command to "greet one another with a holy kiss" (Rom. 16:16) should be seen as teaching the principle of Christian fraternity through the vehicle of the first century ceremony. Teaching passages should generally be regarded as the place to find the meaning of symbolic passages. The teaching language is usually open and plain while the symbols tend to be ambiguous. Doctrines should not be founded on one verse or a few miscellaneous verses. Rather, the general tenor of the Bible should be sought. Inevitably there will be aspects of biblical truth that appear to finite minds to be contradictory. A reverent Bible student will live with these apparently contradictory truths recognizing his finiteness. Basic to all these subordinate emphases is the overarching emphasis of the Bible on God's saving purpose in history. Each part of the Bible must be seen in relation to this organic and teleological purpose. God's saving purpose is an unfolding process. Each event in the Bible has its roots in the past, its meaning in the present, and its development or fulfilment in the future. When the Bible is seen as an organic and unfolding process, even the historical portions and the many incidental events have meaning and importance.

The Practical Meaning

It is obvious that many conflicts arise among Christians in regard to the practical meaning of the Bible. The culmination of biblical interpretation is the application of the biblical message to the modern world. Having found out what it *did* mean, the interpreter must ask, "What *does* it mean?" Some interpreters can make clear what the biblical writers meant in their time. They are aware of the theological convictions which guided the prophets and the apostles. They have less ability, however, to relate this meaning to the contemporary world. Other interpreters conduct contemporary discussions which have little relationship to the biblical meaning and message. An adequate interpreter will seek to present the biblical word as the address of God to men in specific situations today.

His work will result in translation into contemporary idiom. This means that the interpreter must ask the right questions of both the biblical passage and his hearers or readers. Furthermore, he will seek to guide his hearers or readers to a responsible implementation of Bible truth in action.

An Example

Is God literally on a throne a few thousand feet in the air? Isaiah 6:1 describes God with throne, robe, and bodily appearance. Utilizing the doctrine of accommodation suggested by John Calvin four centuries ago, a contemporary interpreter realizes that this was the way God was represented to Isaiah. The truth for then, expressed in eighth century B.C. categories, and for today is that there is a personal God of holiness and transcendence behind the dramatic language. For Isaiah, Calvin, and contemporary men of faith, the use of the upward metaphors to describe God preserves the otherness and transcendence of God. Isaiah's statement will forever refute any monist or mystical identification of God and man such as some Hindus and Buddhists teach today.

In most cases application involves the working out from the passage a principle for life today. Sometimes this is not easy, as Michelsen has shown. When Isaiah saw the Lord high and lifted up, he said, "Here am I; send me (Isa. 6:8)." This passage seems to have an obvious application to life today. Yet in the original context it was necessary for Isaiah to declare that God's decision for judgment had been issued; the days of Israel were numbered. It is not easy to find a parallel situation today. In this connection it should be remembered that a passage should never be used in such a way as to distort the original meaning. 1 Corinthians 11:27, according to the KJV, is translated as, "whosoever shall eat this bread, and drink this cup of the Lord, unworthily, shall be guilty of the body and blood of the Lord." The word "unworthily" is often seen in the wrong light in the KJV translation. Individuals suggest that they are not worthy of partaking of the Lord's Supper. The RSV is more accurate when it translates the original as "in an unworthy manner." In Corinth, the Christians evidently turned the love feast which was climaxed by the Lord's Supper into an orgy. The meaning of this passage for today would involve the precept that the Christian should participate in the Lord's Supper in a reverent and worthy manner with an understanding heart.

The test of a practical application is whether or not it communicates the intention implied in the biblical text. For example, in the first century the resurrection of Christ meant that the new age had begun, Christ had been enthroned, and man could live by the power of the new age here and now. This principle is obviously applicable today, as much as ever before.

Perils of Proof-texting

As indicated above, some people try to regulate details of life from specific texts. Conflict arises when the biblical details are not followed. After the original meaning of a passage has been learned, the interpreter is in a position to apply it to life today. But the emphasis should be on principles and not on specific details. The New Testament writers constantly moved through specifics to principles. It is obvious that no one should try to dress as did first century people or follow their hair styles. Yet the principle of propriety or quiet modesty is involved in the biblical materials which deal with dress and appearance (1 Peter 3:3; 1 Timothy 2:9).

Conflict could be avoided or reduced if the biblical principles outlined above could be seen as more than rigid and mechanical rules. They are helpful guidelines for the Christian as he seeks to improve his biblical understanding and appropriate the resources and guidance which God has given to man in and through the Bible. Improper habits of biblical interpretation should be frankly admitted and rejected. Constant practice and dialogue with other interpreters should be encouraged. In a culture in which dozens of radical cults claim to properly interpret the Bible, it is imperative that attention be given to understanding and putting into practice these generally accepted principles.

Summary

Christians fight over the Bible because they have different approaches and methods to its interpretation. This bewildering variety of interpretation is fruitful of much conflict.

CHAPTER TWELVE

Is the Bible
Historically Conditioned?

A continuing source of conflict between Christians is over the extent of the historical conditioning of Biblical passages and Scriptural teaching.

The *liberals* see extensive conditioning of Bible material. Using form-critical methods, they seek to distinguish between a central core and unhistorical accretions. The Bible, according to Raymond Abba, is both situation-conditioned and time-conditioned. This time-relativity does not apply only to the Old Testament. It also applies to the New Testament.

The teachings of Paul, says Abba, are frequently colored by his prejudices and background. Even Jesus must be seen, according to Abba, as a first century Oriental. He did not know the problems of relativity in politics and the necessary balances of power.

Even Karl Barth apparently suggests that the biblical writers were conditioned by their cultural and historical backgrounds and therefore incapable of seeing the whole truth from their partial viewpoints.

In contrast to liberalism, *conservatives* hold that an objectively inspired Bible gives propositional truths and revealed doctrines. These norms make it possible to give guidance over against the historical relativity of the liberals.

The *New Evangelicals* admit that a certain degree of relativism is necessary and beneficial in understanding the Bible. It would be foolish to think that the biblical writers could be understood without relating them to their particular historical age. But this relativity is limited or it would erode all norms and absolutes and nullify divine authority.

The external form of a passage will naturally reflect the particulars of a certain age. The essential or religious truth is supernatural in nature and origin, and thus is changeless. The inspired Biblical writers were able to transcend their restricting cultural environment when speaking God's Word.

Interpretation is Affected

How do these conflicting views affect interpretations of controversial passages?

Concerning the creation of the world and man, most *liberals* believe that the Bible accounts are conditioned. Under the impact of modern discovery many liberals have become convinced that evolution of some kind is a fact, and they have adjusted their views to this. Evolution became simply the methodology used by God to bring to pass the various forms of life. Instead of creating anew with each species, God used what He had already completed as the basis for the next step in the creative plan. Those who have adopted such a view have usually held that the "days" of Genesis 1 represent long periods of time, or eras. Such an interpretation as this would be in keeping with the order in which plant and animal fossils are said to be found.

God took some higher living primate, and said in effect, "You're it," and did something or added something to this form, making it qualitatively different, and thus constituted him man. An age of the earth of five to six billion years is accepted by the liberals. Some *New*

Evangelicals, such as Ramm and Carnell, have indicated that theistic evolution is not totally contradictory to the biblical account. As indicated above, theistic evolution preaches that God began the process by the first act of creation of matter and energy, and perhaps even life. He then worked creatively from within nature by immanent laws rather than by miraculous special creation. Man's physical makeup developed by a process of evolution. At some point, God took an existing animate form and by some direct creative act implanted in it a spiritual nature. This was referred to as "soul" or the image of God. Man therefore became qualitatively different from what he had been. While neither Ramm nor Carnell have in their writings indicated total acceptance of this view, they indicate that a Bible-believing Christian could accept it if compelled to by the evidence.

The *traditional orthodox* view has assumed that God's creative activity is best explained in terms of the creation of basic kinds or species by an "act of will" on the part of God. Such creative activity is generally viewed as having taken place simultaneously—or at least within a comparatively short period of time, certainly not through a process nor over a span of time involving millions of years.

In regard to the age of the earth, traditional orthodox writers have followed one of two ways to get the necessary amount of time into the biblical record. The *gap theory* inserted the time between verses one and two of Genesis 1. God had made an original creation billions of years ago. Then a catastrophe came, and it became "formless and empty (v. 2)." Beginning in verse 3, we have a description of a re-creation which God performed in six twenty-four-hour days over six thousand years ago. The traditional orthodox strategy has another approach. This approach accounts for the time by means of the flood, at which time conditions were set up which radically altered the earth. Under great pressure, layers of rock were laid down which would ordinarily take long periods of time to form. Thus the earth *appears* to be much older than it actually is.

Many traditionalists assume that the Hebrew word *min,* translated "kind" in most English versions, was to be equated with the biological concept of species. God had at the beginning created all the species which we now have and these have remained fixed to the present time. A traditionalist strategy therefore has been to combat evolution or development of any kind. Since the traditionalist usually held that the flood in Genesis covered the entire earth, there are also some problems in getting at least two specimens of all of the present animal species (except fish and amphibians) into a ship with less than 35,000 square feet of floor space (the Ark).

The *New Evangelicals* accept the biblical description which shows God making man by a definite and distinct act. This was done not only in the classic creation account in Genesis, but in the poetic and prophetic books as well.

The New Evangelicals have abandoned both the gap and flood theories. The most popular alternative among them is the *age-day theory.* This theory maintains that the days in the records of creation in Genesis 1 are not twenty-four hours but long periods of indefinite length. Whereas Fundamentalism had taken the word "day" (*yom* in the Hebrew) in its most literal meaning, the New Evangelicals note that it also is used with other meanings. They feel that the idea of an indefinite period of time is the most adequate for the explanation of the Genesis passage. There is a general correlation between the six creative days of Genesis and the geological periods.

While Bernard Ramm indicates that this was the view which he held for a long time—and he still has great respect for it—his research has moved him to what he refers to as the *"pictorial-day theory."* Ramm suggests that the creation was not performed in six days, but was *revealed* in six days, or under the form of six days. In a series of pictures, God made known to the writer of Genesis the general facts of creation. The grouping may be partly chronological and partly topical. It is not to be taken as a precise description of the order of events or of the amount of time involved.

The New Evangelicals hold to "Progressive creationism." This view states that the word "kind" is not to be identified with "species." It is a general term meaning simply "subdivisions of." What God did was to create a broader grouping, perhaps on the level of the biological order. Over a long period, development took place through implanted laws or principles, and new species arose. Then it was that God initiated another kind and more development occurred. There was evolution within each kind, but not from one kind to another. The term "progressive creationism" denies instantaneous creation and fixity of species but allows for a moderate amount of development. It is creationism, however, because it denies that evolution has been total. God has created by a series of acts.

The New Evangelical apologists believe that this view can be responsible in the light of assured scientific data. The paleontological record reveals a number of gaps in which there are no transitional forms. These are generally at the level of the order. The evolutionist must either say that there have been transitional forms which have now been permanently lost, or state that new forms arose spontaneously (by mutation) which were radically different from any prior forms. The progressive creationist feels that he more adequately accounts for these gaps by correlating with a series of acts of God, by which He made something quite new.

The New Evangelicals are divided as to how to date Adam. Some scholars identify him with early fossil man. This allows a figure as high as a million years. Other scholars place him at about 40,000 years. They maintain either that earlier forms were not human or that they belong to some pre-Adamite race of men. There are some difficulties in any of these interpretations, and for the most part, the evangelicals have left the exact dating of man an open issue.

Perhaps of greater theological importance is the unity of the human race. Are all men descended from a common ancestor, or were there two or more streams of origin of the human race as we know it today? Again, the fossil record gives some divergence of evidence.

It can readily be seen that there is doctrinal significance attached to this point. The apostle Paul argues in Romans 5 that all men are sinners and therefore under condemnation. The reason is that, in Adam, sin entered the race, and all men are descended from Adam. Thus Paul's argument seems to stand or fall with the unity of the human race. If there are men who are not derived from Adam, they may not have Adam's sinful nature and his guilt, and therefore may not be in need of redemption.

The New Evangelicals believe that abandoning the monogenetic theory could have far-reaching consequences for a person's view of man, and for one's view of Scripture. There is some paleontological evidence for the polygenetic view. This view, however, seems in recent years to be less impressive than that for the monogenetic claim. Bernard Ramm argues further than anatomically, physiologically, psychologically, and physically, the human race is one. Therefore he concludes that all men are descended from a common origin or from a single pair.

The Subject of Demons

A controversial area related to historical conditioning in the contemporary world is the subject of demons. When we turn to the New Testament, we discover that every facet of the life and ministry of Jesus was dominated by his belief in the reality of demonic forces. Mark, probably the oldest Gospel, clearly reflects Jesus' concern with the defeat of demonic powers. The driving out of demons was an important part of the early period of Jesus' messianic activity.

Interpreters have explained demon subjection and possession and the demonic exorcism in a number of ways. Some scholars admit that Jesus appears to have believed in Satan and demons. For them, however, this belief represents a mere adaptation to the concepts of the age. It in no way represents the content or main thrust of Jesus' teachings. Jesus' purpose was ethical, and He used the concepts of His time as symbols to serve ethical ends. This is sometimes called the accommodation theory.

A second interpretation is similar to the first theory. It suggests that Jesus was a child of His day and was mistaken in His belief about demons. What the ancients call demon possession is today called mental illness.

George Ladd suggests that there is only one interpretation which does full justice to the Gospel data and to the integrity of Christ's person. This is the view which accepts the existence of demons and demonic possession as an objective reality.

As a caster-out-of-demons and a doer-of-miracles, Jesus does not stand alone in His time. The Hellenistic and Jewish environment is full of miraculous events, miracles of the gods, and miraculous deeds. The miracles of Jesus, however, are to be differentiated from the miracles of His time in several ways. The New Testament miracles of Jesus have nothing to do with the magic or magical means and proceedings as do the majority of the miracles outside of the New Testament. The miracles of Jesus furthermore, are a part of the breaking through of the reign of God, which Jesus brought with His person in proclamation and action. They are the reign of God which overcomes and represses the Satanic-demonic sphere of influence. In this situation, the basic distinction to all other miraculous events appears, although the miracles of Jesus may exhibit a number of parallels.

The miracles have as a supposition the faith of the authors and of those who receive the miracles. The disciples were not able to heal the boy because they lacked faith. Jesus can do no miracles in Nazareth because faith is lacking. By this, magic is removed. It is not the knowledge of magical means, but on the contrary, the personal relation between God and Jesus and between Jesus and men, which accomplishes the miracle without magic compulsion or force.

It should be remembered that many of Christ's miracles were done to authenticate His mission and to demonstrate and prove His Messiahship. The Old Testament had indicated that one way in which His Messiahship could be proved was the fact that He would raise the dead, cast out demons, and heal the sick. After the cross and resurrection, and in the Great Commission Christ placed before His disciples a different emphasis. This time the emphasis was on preaching and teaching. The casting out of demons is not listed as one of the nineteen gifts of the Holy Spirit, even though it might possibly be related to the gift of discernment. This is true even if all of these gifts are accepted as *now* gifts. Some scholars, such as Warfield, believe that the more spectacular gifts were primarily given to authenticate Christianity in the first century.

Is "Holy War" completely time-conditioned as many people say in the twentieth-century? Is nonviolence and love the only unconditioned Bible teaching in relationship to conflict and violence? G. Ernest Wright, the eminent Old Testament scholar, contends that the larger biblical picture of God as Lord is perennially valid. Early Israel's institutuion of Holy War was an agency which the Lord used as a device for implanting Israel in Palestine without conferring moral value on the agent or the institution. Conflict continues as both opportunity for change, growth, and broadening, on the one hand, and judgment for failure, on the other. Love in situations of conflict obviously does not involve surrendering individual integrity, while concern for the needy and for justice to the oppressed may involve the active use of power in ways that cannot be described in every instance as nonviolent. Nonviolence can always be defended in a given instance as the best means to obtain a necessary and quite specific objective. Yet to absolutize it as the only form of action love can take in conflict would be far too limiting for the flexibilites needed to reach God's goals when we are faced with the principalities and powers of darkness. Wright contends that this position is stated in the most general of terms. If this sort of approach caused

Him to give general support of a given war, it would certainly not lead Him to a self-righteous support of a given "just war" theory as background for that war. Wright contends that all wars exemplify human evil in its most virulent expression. Since this is true one can only set up guidelines as limits of coercive action, such as the Geneva Convention.

Summary

Christians fight because they differ over the question of the historical conditioning of the Bible. The issue is more than an abstract and general one; it is expressed in concrete and specific instances such as the validity of war.

CHAPTER THIRTEEN

Differing Views
Of Last Things

In no area is there more conflict than in the interpretation of last things—especially as they are described in the book of Revelation. The sale of over five million copies of Hal Lindsey's *The Late Great Planet Earth* is indicative of popular interest in this area.

There are numerous conflicting views among Christians concerning how to interpret biblical materials about last things.

The *forth-telling*, or "in that history" view, regards the prophecies of the book of Revelation, for example, as wholly concerned with John's own day. Liberal scholars largely endorse this view. They do not accept the book of Revelation as a predictive book. Many liberals, however, accept as valid certain principles of God's moral government taught in the book.

The *historical*, or "all of history" view, sees the visions of the book of Revelation as a preview of history from John's time until the end of the world. The Protestant Reformers had sympathy with this view.

The *poetic*, or "above history" view, sees the prophet describing in a dramatic way the sure triumph of God over all evil powers.

Conservative interpreters are divided into four divisions. All four of these groups are literalists if one is allowed to define the word literal. By literal is meant interpreting words in their normal and proper designa-

tion. There is a division among these conservative interpreters between strict and moderate literalists.

A view popular in the early part of the twentieth century is called postmillennialism. This group is convinced
of the spread of the Christian church by the power of the
Spirit until it brings the millennial condition upon the
earth.

Another view held by many devout and brilliant Bible
scholars is called *amillennialism*. This group believes that
the prophecies made to Israel are fulfilled in the church.
If these prophecies are so fulfilled no millennium on earth
is necessary.

Opponents of this view call it a liberal or allegorical
view, but it must be strongly stated that amillennarians
are just as strong in rejecting baseless allegorical specu-
lations as are the strict literalists. To accuse the amillennarians of being allegorists and implying that their
allegorizations are of the same species as that of Philo or
Origen is simply not being accurate with or fair to the
amillennarians.

Strong Opposition

The opposition among various groups is quite vocal.
Chafer, a dispensational premillennialist, said of the
amillennial method of interpretation that it surpassed
Christian Science and Jehovah's Witnesses in fantastic
imagination and abandonment of simple terms.

George Eldon Ladd, writing in Eternity Magazine,
May, 1964, stated:

"[Amillennialism maintains] that because Israel rejected
her Messiah, God has rejected Israel. So the Kingdom has
been taken away from Israel and 'given to a nation bringing forth the fruits thereof' (Matt. 21:43). This 'royal
priesthood,' this 'holy nation,' this 'peculiar people' is the

Church (1 Pet. 2:9). The Church is therefore the spiritual Israel, the true people of God.

"According to this view, the Church is now the 'Israel of God' (Gal. 6:16). The spiritual Israel has taken the place of the literal Israel. The Old Testament promises to the literal Israel must be interpreted in terms of the spiritual blessings enjoyed by the Church. Therefore there is no need of a Millennial Kingdom. Israelites will be saved only as they believe on Christ and come into the Church."

Dispensational Premillennialism

The view, popularized in Hal Lindsey's *The Late Great Planet Earth*, is called "Dispensational Premillennialism." This view insists upon a rigid application of an exact literal interpretation, particularly as it has to do with Israel, the church, and the future.

Dispensationalism holds that [Ladd] "Israel and the Church are two separate peoples which cannot be mingled and must not be confused. In fact, according to this view, God has two different programs which he is carrying out in history: one with Israel and one with the Church. God's theocratic program with Israel was interrupted when Israel rejected Christ. God therfore turned away from Israel to accomplish His redemptive purpose in the Church. When this purpose has been fulfilled, God will resume His relations with Israel. The Millennium will see the resumption of this theocratic purpose and Israel will be restored as a nation in her land of Palestine with a reconstituted monarchy, and will rule over the nations of the earth on behalf of her God. Her King will be the promised Davidic Messiah who will sit upon the literal throne of David and rule the world from Jerusalem. Israel's temple worship and priestly order of Old Testament times, including the sacrificial system, will be restored. All the promises of the Old Testament will be fulfilled in literal terms. The Millennium, in other words, will be a revival or renewal of the Old Testament order. The church age is a parenthesis in God's program for Israel and must not be confused with it."

This view divides the Scriptures according to classes of people (Israel or the Church). It insists that no single passage can have primary application to two dispensations at the same time. The Pre-Tribulation Rapture grows out of their concept of the Church—it cannot be on the earth when God's earthly purposes commence again to restore the literal earthly reign of Christ according to the Abrahamic and Davidic covenant. The Pre-Tribulational Rapture view is Dispensational, rooted in the principle of interpretation which separates the church from the total redemptive plan of God. The church must be raptured out of the world before the tribulation because it is not part of the kingdom, which will be in its initial stage of restoration through the remnant that survives the tribulation.

The church is removed from the earth in the Rapture. The seven-year period which follows is divided into two three-and-one-half-year periods, during the first of which Israel enters into a covenant with the antichrist, who breaks it at the end. The second half-period begins when Satan overpowers the antichrist and the "time of Jacob's trouble" is poured out on the world. During the seven years of tribulation the gospel of the kingdom (notice: Not the gospel of grace) is preached. An elect remnant of Israel, numbering 144,000, survives the tribulation to become the kingdom to which Christ returns after the seven years.

The millennial reign is decidedly Jewish; the consummation of God's plan for Israel; the literal fulfilment of Old Testament prophecy. Christ will be on a physical throne and all nations subservient to Israel.

Some say the church will return at the beginning and pass through, but others say it is a part of the holy city hovering above the earth. The Temple is to be rebuilt, and the sacrifices are to be re-instituted. The relation of this sacrificial system to the death of Christ is "commemorative," not anticipatory. The blessed hope for the dispensationalists, seemingly, is that Christ will rapture the parenthetical church so that He may reign through Israel, not the church.

The organized church on earth is apostate. Dispensationalists early distinguished between the "true church" and Christendom, the organized church. The "true church" was composed only of the saved. Only a few out of many professing Christians are included. Thus the "true church" could be described only in terms of the relation of the believer, not in terms of the organized structure.

Hal Lindsey, in *The Late Great Planet Earth,* supplies a concrete future referent for each symbol in the book of Revelation. John, according to Lindsey, sees the future historical events as God reveals them. However, John is "unsophisticated" concerning IBM's and other nuclear warfare weapons. So John describes "these things" as best he can. For example, the hail and fire of Revelation 8:7 probably point to an IBM. A locust with the face of a man, the teeth of a lion, a breastplate of iron, a tail that can sting, and wings that make the sound of many chariots might symbolize an advanced kind of helicopter. The "two wings of a great eagle" in Revelation 12:14 could be "aircraft from the United States Sixth Fleet in the Mediterranean."

Historical Premillennialism

The last view to be considered is advocated by most of the new evangelicals such as George Ladd and Daniel Fuller. This view is called "Historical Premillennialism." It is a view mediating between amillennialism and dispensationalism.

Historical premillennialism accepts the view held by the amillennialists that the Church [again quoting Ladd's *Eternity* article] "has taken the place of Israel and must be called the 'spiritual' Israel. This 'spiritualizing' of Israel began in the Old Testament. Paul makes this clear. Not all who are descended from Abraham *physically* are sons of Abraham *spiritually*. 'Neither, because they are the seed of Abraham, are they all children' (Rom. 9:7). 'They which are the children of the flesh, these are not the children of God; but the children of the promise are counted for the seed' (Rom. 9:8). The physical seed is not the true seed. The literal Israel is not the spiritual Israel. The Scripture limits the true spiritual seed of Abraham to one narrowing line within the physical descendants.

"Not only is the spiritual seed of Abraham limited to a small group within the literal seed, it is also extended to the Church. Paul makes this clear in Romans 4:16 and 18. God had promised Abraham that his seed should be as innumerable as the stars; Paul applies this promise to the Church. This promise to Abraham's seed, says Paul, was given 'not to that only which is of the law [the literal seed] but to that also which is of the faith of Abraham' [the spiritual seed] (Rom. 4:16). Therefore, 'if ye be Christ's, then are ye Abraham's seed, and heirs according to the promise' (Gal. 3:29).

"Thus Abraham is 'the father of us all' who have the same justifying faith which Abraham had (Rom. 4:16). Abraham has been made 'the father of all them that believe, though they be not circumcised' (Rom. 4:11). Abraham's spiritual seed, his true spiritual children, are the men of faith—believers in the Lord Jesus Christ—the Church. Thus the Church in a real sense *is* the spiritual Israel."

Views Combined

The Historic-Premillennial view seeks to combine the forth-telling and fore-telling views of the book of Revelation. The beast of Revelation 13, is reflected first in the Roman Emperor but finally presented as a personal Antichrist in the time of the end. Revelation 19 describes in apocalyptic symbolic terms the Second Coming of Christ to destroy the satanic evil embodied in Rome and Antichrist. This is pictured as a bloody battle, but the only weapon is the Word proceeding from the mouth of the conquering Messiah (Rev. 19:15). The millennium is one interval in the accomplishing of God's redemptive rule (the Kingdom of God).

Millennium

Again to quote Ladd, for the Historic Premillennialist: "The New Testament provides us with a few glimpses of the fact that the two days are really three; that beyond the second coming is a further extension of Christ's reign over the world before the *telos*. The millennium is a manifestation of God's redemptive rule in Christ by which his enemies will finally be destroyed. God has not seen fit through the prophetic Scriptures to answer all the questions we may have about these future events, but He has provided the main outlines of the consummation of his redemptive purpose." *(Revelation 20 and the Millen-*
[*Telos* is new heaven and new earth.]

Daniel Fuller

Daniel Fuller, reared in a dispensational premillennial home, changed to historic premillennialism after long study. The problem with dispensationalism as he came to see it is its *hermeneutical point of departure*. It assumes two peoples of God. Though it finds a basis in some passages for making the status of Israel and the Church antithetical, it does not stand up well with what the Bible *as a whole* says. It assumes too quickly the eternal distinction between the two peoples of God. Therefore the interpreter enters a vicious circle: having accepted a controlling idea before listening to all that the Bible says on the subject, he then becomes less able to hear the overall message of the Bible, for he has made the decision to compartmentalize it.

Problem with Literalism

It is admitted by Fuller that dispensationalists have a deep love for the Bible. However, he contends that their rigid literalism is not consistent, and that it destroys the unity of the Bible. Therefore such a system, which is both internally inconsistent and unable to harmonize itself with the biblical data, must be based on a faulty hermeneutical basis.

Clarence Bass

Another New Evangelical, Clarence Bass, contends that dispensational premillennialism has caused many people to withdraw from the larger fellowship in Christ. George Eldon Ladd suggests that if dispensationalists would accept their system as but one of several options within orthodox theology and would be willing to enter into fraternal charitable dialogue with other positions, a new day would dawn in American evangelicalism.

This is not a complete depiction of all the varying views. What we have presented is enough of the issue, told in enough detail to indicate how complicated a controversy can easily arise in this area.

Summary

Differing views of the millennial issue lead to much conflict among sincere Christians over the Bible.

CHAPTER FOURTEEN

Differing Views of
Higher Criticism

In no area is there more emotion and conflict between Christians than in the area of higher criticism of the Bible. Unfortunately, the words "Biblical criticism" have come to have negative connotations because of the theological position of many people engaged in the study—especially in earlier years. These critics were seen to regard the Bible as a purely human historical product. If this is the definition accepted, it is understandable why conservative Christians have been hostile to it. As a result of this background, new evangelicals such as George Ladd are suggesting that the term "historical-theological criticism," which recognizes the revelatory dimension in biblical history and the revelatory nature of the Bible, be used. This is a better term, they suggest, than the traditional term "historical-critical method," which has been developed by rationalistic scholarship.

The liberals contend that behind the written accounts found in the Bible stands an oral stage of transmission. Richard J. Coleman, among others, has set forth the liberal position with clarity.

This oral period is seen as dynamic and formative. In the case of the Old Testament separate oral traditions had been in existence for centuries. Different traditions grew up and centered around important heroic figures such as Moses, Joshua, and David. Traditions also grew up around certain clutic centers such as Bethel, Shiloh, and Hebron. At a later time, basic theological motifs emerged, such as the election of Israel, Exodus, and law-giving. The final step was taken by a redactor or author who put the written documents into the final form we find in the Bible. Throughout all this process, there was an element of selection at work. The community only preserved the elements of the tradition that it found use-ful for its own self-understanding. The high critics find the same basic process operating in the New Testament although it is telescoped into a shorter period. The life of Jesus was not written down immediately nor was it passed along orally as a connected whole. An exception of this might have been the Passion narrative. Traditions about Jesus were preserved in smaller individual units sometimes called Pericopes. These are classified as say-ings, short stories, legends and teaching materials such as the parables. A final author collected and shaped the various traditions into a coherent whole.

The liberals see that the written word was not as im-portant to the early church people as was the spoken word. The biblical writers were first preachers and the-ologians. They were primarily concerned with passing on an oral tradition rather than writing down the tradition.

A more radical form critic such as Ernst Käsemann contends that the work of the form critics has shown that the message of Jesus as given to us by the Gospel writers, is for the most part, not authentic. It was treated by the faith of the primitive Christian community in its various stages. In fairness, it should be said that not all form critics find such a complete transformation of the gospel tradi-tion. Vincent Taylor, for example, is an English scholar who has written in the area of form criticism. He holds a rather high view of the trustworthiness of the historical tradition. It must be said, however, that there are many people who have a more radical tradition. The opposite extreme is illustrated by Rudolf Bultmann who had concluded that the nature of our Gospels is such that we can now know almost nothing about the life and personality of Jesus.

The liberal scholars teach that the biblical writers used great freedom in compiling the biblical books as has already been mentioned. The biblical authors were men with distinctive personalities who employed a number of literary devices to achieve their particular purposes. They did their own thing. They would select Old Testament passages, expand materials, stylize it, utilize different settings, and also use catchword linkings. German scholars such as Jeremias and Bornkamm illustrate this approach in their writings. The author of the Gospel of John is oftentimes cited as an author who obviously did not attempt to relate the exact words of Jesus. He demonstrated a high degree of creativity in reinterpreting the traditions about Jesus in order to bring out what he considered to be the truth of the gospel. Matthew organized the teaching materials of Jesus into sections. Paul showed no compulsion to relate the words of Jesus and used terminology so different that he has been accused of preaching a different gospel.

Liberals conclude that the church, like Israel, was untroubled by differences in detail or emphasis in parallel traditions and did not see these differences as errors or contradictions which gave them difficulty.

An illustration of how the form critics deal with material can be seen in the way they handle a pericope or unit about the founding of the church which is found in Matthew 16:17,19. They contend that this unit cannot be historical, for the "historical Jesus" did not think of Himself as a person with a divine mission to bring into existence

a new people—the church. Jesus saw Himself as an apocalyptic Jewish prophet whose mission and message were
concerned only with the Jewish people. Matthew 16:17–
19 represents an attempt by the church to justify its existence by an unhistorical attributing of its ultimate origin
to Jesus. The life situation of this passage is not the life
and teachings of the historical Jesus but the Christian
church which believed itself to be the church, the new
people of God, founded by Jesus.

It is also interesting to see how the form critics deal with
verses such as Mark 13:10 and Matthew 24:14. These
verses place on the lips of Jesus a prophecy of the worldwide Christian mission. The critics say these cannot be
historically reliable, for Jesus could not foresee the future.
Furthermore, He did not believe that the world would
last long and had no purpose to found a church. This
again is only a saying created by Christian tradition to
vindicate its own mission in the Gentile world by attributing it to Jesus.

It can be seen that at the hands of extreme form critics,
the Gospels lose much of their trustworthiness as historical records, and the picture of Jesus is lost. The Son of
God incarnate in Jesus of Nazareth becomes a product
rather than the creator of the Christian faith. He is no
longer seen as the Saviour of the Christian community. It
is not surprising that evangelicals with a high view of the
Bible and of Christ have felt that form criticism is nothing
but an enemy of the Christian faith as evangelicals have
come to understand it. It can be seen that for the liberals
a history of Jesus, like the history of Israel, is really more
the product of faith than it is the product of eye witness
reports. The concern of the New Testament writers was
not to preserve Jesus in written word, but to proclaim
Him. It was only as expectation of His early return began

to fade, about A.D. 60, that the written gospels began to take shape. It still was not an historical interest, but the theological interest that brought the Gospels into existence according to the liberals. It was also their natural inclination of the Bible authors to read their faith back into the original accounts. For them to heighten, change, enlarge, and reinterpret the material was not regarded as disrespectful. They saw it as necessary to keep the memory of Christ alive. In this way the preachers and proclaimers became a part of the message proclaimed. Even as they did then, today we can only see the Jesus of history through the eyes of faith.

Each of the Gospel writers, such as Mark and John, are seen as writing from a particular theological viewpoint into which he arranged geographical and chronological information. Behind every emphasis and every variation in detail, there was some theological concern. Hans Conzelmann brings this out in a dramatic way in his book *The Theology of St. Luke.*

The conservative has great misgivings about the basic views of the liberals regarding higher criticism. Conflict is in the air at many levels of discussion.

Traditional conservatives have long held that Moses wrote the first five books of the Old Testament and the disciples and other eyewitnesses wrote the Gospels. For the conservative, the written word has supremacy over the oral word. The conservative points out that archeological evidence shows that writing was known in the time of Moses. He contends that the biblical writers were concerned to preserve an accurate account of what took place. The early church, for example, recorded the record of Jesus' life not only because it was useful but because of an interest in Jesus himself. Archeology has also shown many examples from the Near East of cultures that wrote down their traditions while they were still flourishing in oral form. It is also pointed out by the conservatives that the ancient people were very reliable in preserving unchanged materials passed on by word of mouth. Those who go to the Middle East today know something of their accuracy, their monotonous style, and their use of rhythm and euphony to preserve the exact details. In the Jewish world, the rabbinic way of life was also committed to passing on exact wording as well as the exact thought. In fact, there were many safeguards. Only properly trained rabbis and pupils were allowed to pass down tradition. Traditional conservatives such as Clark Pinnock point out that Christianity was born as a book-religion. Although some parts were passed on orally, the natural disposition was to trust the written word. It is only in the written word that the sacred words could be preserved from error and copied without limitation.

New Evangelicals will admit that there is some truth in form criticism. It is quite certain that the gospel was in fact preserved for a generation in oral form before it was reduced to writing, according to George Ladd. When an examination is made of the prologue of Luke's Gospel, it is noted that Luke distinguishes between his own Gospel, other written records, and those things which were delivered to Luke by eyewitnesses and ministers of the word. This description is found in Luke 1:1,2.

The redemptive events recorded in the Gospels are "objective" in the sense that they really happened in time and space. Their nature, however, is such that they stand apart from merely human "historical" events, even though they occurred in history. They cannot be understood by ordinary human observation but only by the response of faith. The experience of Paul illustrates this fact. Paul's faith did not change the human Jesus into a divine redeemer. On the contrary, it was faith which enabled Paul to understand who Jesus really was.

The admission that only faith could write a gospel does not necessitate the conclusion that such faith cannot be "objective." Admitting the importance of faith does not result inevitably in a distortion of the facts in its own interests. On the contrary, only faith can really recognize what the facts really were. The New Testament teaches that the disciples did not truly understand who Jesus was until after the resurrection. It was only as they looked back to what Jesus had said and done, and viewed His person and deeds and words in the light of their resurrection faith, that they saw that He was indeed the Son of God in power. It was only then that they could correctly understand why He had acted as He had.

The New Evangelicals will agree with the form critics that the Gospels are not "neutral, objective" records but are the products of the Christian faith. The New Evangelicals further assert, however, that this fact in no way renders the Gospels untrustworthy. On the contrary, it is only a historical criticism which is tempered by faith that can really recognize what God has done in history in Jesus of Nazareth. Evangelicals will admit that the Bible contains a combination of history and interpretation. But at the same time, this admission does not imply that the authors presumed on their own initiative to alter or add to the material which they had in order to change or improve the Word of God. It has always been the evangelical perspective that the Holy Spirit made possible the element of interpretation which was woven into the history that constitutes the Gospel tradition. This interpretive material, however, simply draws out the implications of history rather than imposing something new upon it.

Evangelicals will admit that each Gospel should be

studied in terms of its supposed life situation. It does not follow, however, that this life situation exercised a significant creative factor in the formation of the content of the Gospel tradition. It is important to note that the biblical authors were conscious of their own illumination and of the inspired nature of the material which they were preserving. They handled tradition, both oral and written, guided by an awareness that they were speaking not for themselves but for God and by the Holy Spirit. Matthew and Luke, for example, deliberately arrange their materials not in terms of how they think the events they record happened historically, but in terms of the portrait of Jesus' person, mission, and message that the Spirit guided them to sketch. Paul spoke and wrote with authority only because he was conscious of his apostolic calling to make the word of God fully known among the Gentiles.

Conservatives see the liberal view denying to the Christian world any direct access to historical facts by their over-emphasis on subjective interpretation. The fact is that eyewitnesses were present for many years after the ascension of Christ. Jesus, Himself, had a strong Messianic consciousness and taught the disciples basic truths for future generations. There was evidently frequent discussion of the Christian tradition in the various Christian communities between Peter and other leaders.

It is also noteworthy that traditions were preserved and preached which were not popular and which in turn caused division.

Conservatives contend that the New Testament records faithfully reflect the teaching of Jesus. This does not mean that conservatives will reject historical criticism. Since revelation occurred in historical events, the student of the Bible must use historical techniques to understand these events in terms of their historical setting. But the historical method should not be allowed to determine the nature of revelation. If revelation has occurred in historical events, it is not surprising that there is a dimension in these redemptive events which transcends or goes beyond the historical method. The Christian student, however, must not allow the modern historian to dictate to him the limits of its discipline. George Ladd, a well-known New Evangelical, contends that only the believing historian can adequately understand what God has done in history. He sees that this is in agreement with the witness of Scripture itself, which says, "If you believe in your heart that God raised him from the dead, you will be saved" (Rom. 10:9).

Bibliography

Abba, Raymond, *The Nature and Authority of the Bible.* Philadelphia: Muhlenberg Press, 1958.

Arndt, W., *Bible Difficulties.* St. Louis, Missouri: Concordia, 1971.

Averill, Lloyd J., *American Theology in the Liberal Tradition.* New York: Doubleday, 1969.

Barth, Markus, *Conversation with the Bible.* New York, Chicago, San Francisco: Holt, Rinehart and Winston, 1964.

Barr, James, *Old and New in Interpretation.* New York: Harper, 1966.

Bass, Clarence B., *Backgrounds to Dispensationalism.* Grand Rapids, Michigan: Wm. B. Eerdmans, 1960.

Beasley, George R.-Murray, *Highlights of the Book of Revelation.* Nashville, Tennessee: Broadman Press, 1972.

Bloesch, Donald G. *The Evangelical Renaissance.* Grand Rapids, Michigan: William B. Eerdmans Publishing Company, 1973.

Bornkamm, Gunther, Barth, Gerhard, and Held, Heinz, J., *Tradition and Interpretation in Matthew,* Trans. Percy Scott, Philadelphia: Westminster, 1963.

Braaten, Carl E., *New Directions in Theology Today.* Volume II. History and Hermeneutics. Philadelphia: The Westminster Press, 1966.

Bright, John, *The Authority of the Old Testament*. Nashville: Abingdon, 1967.

Bultmann, Rudolph, *Is Exegesis without Presuppositions Possible?,*" Existence and Faith. Cleveland: World, 1960.

Carnell, Edward J., *The Case for Orthodox Theology*. Philadelphia: Westminster, 1959.

Cartledge, Samuel A., *The Bible: God's Word to Man*. Philadelphia: The Westminster Press, 1961.

Clark, Gordon, *A Christian View of Men and Things*. Grand Rapids: Eerdmans, 1952.

Clark, Gordon H., *Religion, Reason and Revelation*. Philadelphia, Pennsylvania: Presbyterian and Reformed Publishing Company, 1961.

Coleman, Richard J., *Issues of Theological Warfare: Evangelicals and Liberals*. Grand Rapids, Michigan: William B. Eerdmans Publishing Company, New Edition, 1972.

Conzelmann, Hans, *The Theology of St. Luke*, Trans. Geoffrey Buswell. New York: Harper, 1961.

Criswell, W.A. *The Bible for Today's World*. Grand Rapids, Michigan: Zondervan Publishing House, 1966.

Criswell, W.A. *Why I Preach That the Bible Is Literally True*. Nashville: Broadman, 1969.

Ebeling, Gerhard, "The Significance of the Critical Historical Method for Church and Theology in Protestantism," *Word and Faith*. Philadelphia: Fortress, 1963.

Erickson, Millard, *The New Evangelical Theology*. Westwood, New Jersey: Revell, 1968.

Gilkey, Langdon, *Naming the Whirlwind: The Renewal of God-Language*. Indianapolis: Bobbs-Merrill, 1969.

Hadden, Jeffrey K., *The Gathering Storm in the Churches*. Garden City, New York: Doubleday, 1969.

Hamilton, Kenneth, *Words and the Word*. Grand Rapids,

Michigan: William B. Eerdmans Publishing Co., 1971.

Henry, Carl F.H., *Evangelicals at the Brink of Crisis.* Waco: Word Books, 1967.

Henry, Carl F.H., *Frontiers in Modern Theology.* Chicago: Moody Press, 1966.

Henry, Carl F.H., *Revelation and the Bible.* Grand Rapids, Michigan: Baker Book House, 1958.

Hordern, William, *Speaking of God. The Nature and Purpose of Theological Language.* New York: The Macmillan Co., London: Collier-Macmillan, 1964.

Kallas, James, *Revelation: God and Satan in the Apocalypse.* Minneapolis, Minnesota: Augsburg Publishing House, 1973.

Käsemann, Ernst, *New Testament Questions of Today,* trans. W.J. Montague. Philadelphia: Fortress, 1969.

Kraus, Norman C., *Dispensationalism in America: Its Rise and Development.* Richmond, Virginia: John Knox Press, 1958.

Kuitert, H.M., *The Reality of Faith: A Way Between Protestant Orthodoxy and Existential Theology,* Trans. L.B. Smedes. Grand Rapids: Eerdmans, 1968.

Kuitert, H.M., *Do You Understand What You Read? On Understanding and Interpreting the Bible.* Translated by Lewis B. Smedes. Grand Rapids, Michigan: William B. Eerdmans Publishing Company, 1970.

Ladd, George E., *The New Testament and Criticism.* Grand Rapids: Eerdmans, 1967.

Ladd, George E., *The Blessed Hope.* Grand Rapids, Michigan: Wm. B. Eerdmans Publishing Company, 1956.

Ladd, George E., *Jesus and the Kingdom. The Eschatology of Biblical Realism.* New York, Evanston, and London: Harper & Row, 1964.

Lindblom, J., *The Bible: A Modern Understanding.*

Trans. by Eric H. Wahlstrom. Philadelphia: Fortress Press, 1969.

Lindsey, Hal, Carlson, C.C., *The Late Great Planet Earth*. Grand Rapids, Michigan: Zondervan Publishing House, 1970.

Lindsey, Hal, *There's a New World Coming. 'A Prophetic Odyssey'*. Santa Ana, California: Vision House Publishers, 1973.

Macquarrie, John, *The Scope of Demythologizing*. London: SCM, 1960.

Mickelsen, Berkeley A., *Interpreting the Bible*. Grand Rapids, Michigan: Wm. B. Eerdmans Publishing Company, 1959.

Miller, Donald G., *The Authority of the Bible*. Grand Rapids, Michigan: William B. Eerdmans Publishing Company, 1972.

Montgomery, John Warwick, *Crisis in Lutheran Theology, The Validity and Relevance of Historic Lutheranism vs. Its Contemporary Rivals*. Vol. I. Minneapolis, Minnesota: Bethany Fellowship, Inc., 1973.

Nash, Ronald H., *The New Evangelicalism*. Grand Rapids, Michigan: Zondervan Publishing House, 1963.

Newport, John P., *Demons, Demons, Demons. A Christian Guide Through the Murky Maze of the Occult*. Nashville, Tennessee: Broadman Press, 1970.

Niebuhr, Richard, *The Meaning of Revelation*. New York: Macmillan, 1941.

Orr, James, *The Christian View of God and the World*. Grand Rapids, Michigan: Eerdmans, 1947.

Pache, Rene, *The Inspiration and Authority of Scripture*. Trans. by Helen I. Needham. Chicago: Moody, 1969.

Packer, J.I., *"Fundamentalism" and the Word of God*. London: Intervarsity Fellowship, 1958.

Pinnock, Clark H., *Biblical Revelation—The Foundation of Christian Theology*. Chicago: Moody Press, 1971.

Ramm, Bernard, *Special Revelation and the Word of God*. Grand Rapids, Michigan: William B. Eerdmans Publishing Co., 1961.

Ramm, Bernard, "The Evidence of Prophecy and Miracle," Revelation and the Bible. Ed., Carl F. H. Henry. Grand Rapids: Baker, 1958.

Ramm, Bernard, *Hermeneutics*. Grand Rapids, Michigan: Baker Book House, 1967.

Ramm, Bernard, *Protestant Biblical Interpretation. A Textbook of Hermeneutics*. Third Revised Edition. Grand Rapids, Michigan: Baker Book House, 1970.

Ramm, Bernard, *The Evangelical Heritage*. Waco, Texas: Word Books, Publisher, 1973.

Ramsey, Ian T., *Religious Language*. New York: Macmillan, 1963.

Ridderbos, Herman N. *The Authority of the New Testament Scriptures*. Trans. by H. De Jongste. Grand Rapids, Michigan: Baker Book House, 1963.

Robinson, John A.T. *Honest to God*. Philadelphia: Westminster, 1963.

Runia, Klass. *Karl Barth's Doctrine of Holy Scripture*. Grand Rapids, Michigan: William B. Eerdmans Publishing Company, 1962.

Sandeen, Ernest R., *The Origins of Fundamentalism*. Philadelphia: Fortress, 1968.

Sandeen, Ernest R. *The Roots of Fundamentalism*. Chicago: University of Chicago, 1970.

Schaeffer, Francis A. *The God Who Is There*. Speaking Historic Christianity into the Twentieth Century. Chicago, Illinois: Inter-Varsity Press, 1968.

Schaeffer, Francis A. *He is There and He Is Not Silent.* Wheaton, Illinois: Tyndale House Publishers, 1972.

Shelley, Bruce. *Evangelicalism in America.* Grand Rapids, Michigan: Eerdmans, 1967.

Smart, James D. *The Interpretation of Scripture.* Philadelphia: The Westminster Press, 1961.

Smart, James, *The Strange Silence of the Bible in the Church.* A Study in Hermeneutics. Philadelphia: The Westminster Press, 1970.

Stevick, Daniel B., *Beyond Fundamentalism.* Richmond, Virginia: John Knox Press, 1964.

Stibbs, Alan M., *Understanding God's Word.* Chicago, Illinois: Inter-Varsity Press, 1956.

Taylor, Vincent, *The Formation of the Gospel Tradition.* London: Macmillan, 1933.

Tenney, Merrill C., (ed.), *The Bible—The Living Word of Revelation.* Grand Rapids, Michigan: Zondervan Publishing House, 1968.

Tenney, Merrill C., (ed.), *The Word for This Century.* New York: Oxford University Press, 1960.

Thielicke, Helmut, *Between Heaven and Earth. Conversations with American Christians.* Trans. and ed. by John W. Doberstein. New York, Evanston, and London: Harper & Row Publishers, 1965.

Thielicke, Helmut, *Man in God's World.* Trans. and ed. by John W. Doberstein. New York, Evanston, and London: Harper & Row Publishers, 1963.

Walvoord, John F., (ed.), *Inspiration and Interpretation.* Grand Rapids, Michigan: Zondervan, 1957.

Wright, G. Ernest, *The Old Testament and Theology.* New York, Evanston, and London: Harper & Row Publishers, 1969.

Appendix

Personality Characteristics
As Psychologists See Them

This book has dealt with its subject from a religious perspective. For a contrasting perspective, recent psychological studies concerning personality characteristics might be explored.

Milton Rokeach in the book *The Open and Closed Mind* comes to the conclusion that there are basically three *regions of belief* in man. He calls these: (1) the central; (2) the intermediate; (3) the peripheral. The central region relates particularly to the self and to the nature of the world in which the self lives. A threat to beliefs in this region is taken very, very seriously. The intermediate region of belief has to do with authority and with authority figures. Beliefs held here are strong ones, but they are not held as strongly as in the central region. Peripheral beliefs matter little except to the extremely dogmatic person.

Rokeach contends that the individual with an open mind is able to bring various belief structures together for comparison purposes. He has an optimistic attitude about the way in which the world is put together, doubts if decisions made today will hold forever, and does not consider authorities to be absolute determiners of policy. His opposite number, the dogmatic person, tends to compartmentalize the various kinds of beliefs he holds and to be very reluctant to compare various beliefs. He is inclined to be more pessimistic about the future of the world. He believes in the absolute correctness of various authorities. He is inclined to reject the ideas of individuals who do not agree with the particular set of authorities in whom he trusts. He takes a very narrow view of the problems of the world.

T. W. Adorno and his associates, in the book *The Authoritarian Personality*, concludes that a person with an authoritarian personality relies heavily on the moral authorities of his own membership group. He tends to adhere rigidly to middle-class values and is preoccupied both with his own relative power and status and with that of those around him. He tends toward absolute judgments in the values he holds. He is not swayed by messages that contradict the authorities he trusts. He identifies himself with those in his own group and tends to be hostile to outsiders.

Joseph A. Ilardo, writing in *The Journal of Communication*, tackles the problem of ambiguity tolerance from the standpoint that too much information input is the primary cause of uncertainty and ambiguity. According to Ilardo, the first response is to increase the information input in the confidence that increased information will bring order out of the chaos. This, of course, is to take a risk, but according to the psychologists it is the healthy response to ambiguity. The second response is to limit the information coming into the system. This is both natural and human. If it is made, the person may employ four methods to limit information. (1) He may simply cut himself off physically from the information. (2) He may withdraw by using the formal institutions of society, such as commitment to a political party. (3) He may make informal or unconscious commitments, such as adopting a restrictive life style. (4) He may use language to limit his range of information and anxiety—as in oversimplification, literalness, and two-valued orientation. People oversimplify in order to avoid doubt. Highly literal persons have rigidity of thought, highly developed organizational abilities, attention to particulars, and ability to think theoretically at high levels of abstraction. They possess minimal originality, novelty, creativity, and spontaneity. They tend to opt for discursive logic which involves explicit meanings over creative fantasy which involves implicit meanings. They tend to see everything in black or white, with no shades of gray.

Needless to say, the personality characteristics of an individual are independent of his position to the right or left. An authoritarian person can be either liberal or conservative. So might a non-authoritarian.

Consideration of personality characteristics is peripheral to the discussion in this book, but it is easy to see how an unfortunate combination of opposing characteristics in opponents might escalate what might have been expected conflict into bitter strife.

Humorous Misuse
Of the Scriptures

Childbirth

Historically, many misuses of Scripture were humorous and even sometimes beneficial. In England when chloroform was developed the doctors wanted to use it on women in child birth. However, women were resistant because 1) Jesus refused the sop offered to him; therefore, they should not take anything to lessen the pain; 2) Genesis 3:16 expressly states that in pain a women should bring forth children. But J.Y. Simpson, who was professor of midwifery at Edinburgh, effectively eliminated their objections on Scriptural grounds by showing from Genesis 2:21 that God "caused a deep sleep to fall upon Adam" in order to create women.

Energy Crisis

When the first oil wells were dug in Pennsylvania, many New York ministers opposed the project. It was argued (from 2 Peter 3:10,12) that to do such a thing was contrary to the Providence of God since it would deplete the oil stored there for the predestined burning of the world.

A Fast Mass

In the Gospel of John 13:27, after Jesus had singled out the traitor, says, ". . . what you are going to do, do quickly". This passage became a suitable proof-text for

Cardinal Newman's admonition to his priests that they should practice a rapid recital of the words of the Mass.

No Fans Please

James Meilkle invented winnowing fans in Scotland in 1710. However, they were generally rejected many years after that because Christians believed that to produce wind by mechanical means was interfering with the Providence of God, for John 3:8 clearly says, "The wind blows where it wills. . . ."

Polygamy

John Milton defended polygamy on Scriptural grounds to the consternation of his Puritan contemporaries. His exhortation was to follow the example of Abraham and Jacob as normative for the Christian age. Even M. Luther reluctantly consented to the bigamous marriage of Phillip of Hesse. The logic was that, since God approved it in the time of the men of faith such as David and Solomon, then it must be right for us also. "A social system which was right in one age cannot be wrong in another."

House-top Preaching

In 1946, Rev. W. Hainsworth of Dexter, Michigan, became disturbed by the apathy of his church members and the general spiritual lethargy of the community. Finally, one Sunday he announced to his people that he was taking a thirty day leave of absence for an itinerant preaching ministry from city to city in order to awaken sinners and Christians alike. Furthermore, he was going to follow Matthew 10:27, "What you hear privately, proclaim upon the housetops," and his preaching tour would be done from roof to roof.

The "Privilege" of Prostitution

In Matthew 21:31 Jesus says, "Truly, I say to you, the tax collectors and the harlots go into the Kingdom of God before you." On the basis of this Scripture, a radical wing of the Anabaptists in Münster encouraged sexual promiscuity as the quickest way into heaven.